Simple Home Cooking

Tapas

D1390633

Publisher & Creative Director: Nick Wells
Senior Project Editor: Marcus Hardy
Art Director: Mike Spender
Layout Design: Jane Ashley
Digital Design & Production: Chris Herbert
Proofreader: Dawn Laker

This is a **FLAME TREE** Book

FLAME TREE PUBLISHING
Crabtree Hall, Crabtree Lane
Fulham, London SW6 6TY
United Kingdom
www.flametreepublishing.com

Flame Tree is part of Flame Tree Publishing Limited

First published 2013

Copyright © 2013 Flame Tree Publishing

13 15 17 16 14
1 3 5 7 9 10 8 6 4 2

Hardback ISBN: 978-0-85775-659-6
Paperback ISBN: 978-0-85775-837-8

A copy of the CIP data for this book is available from the British Library.

Printed in Singapore

Images are courtesy of **Shutterstock.com** and © the following contributors:
1 & 29t JIANG HONGYAN; 3 & 32t, 39b Gayvoronskaya_Yana; 4 & 127, 20t, 20b, 22b, 32c, 44t, 77, 89, 105, 113, 117, 131, 143, 187, 189, 193, 207, 217, 243, 251 nito; 8 SandiMako; 9 Pedro Salaverría; 10 carlosdelacalle; 12 Ashiga; 13 pio3; 14b Fotomicar; 14t Tupungato; 15, 79, 147, 169, 171, 181, 221 Olaf Speier; 16 Foodpictures; 17 & 183, 47, 51 & 159, 61, 65, 69, 71, 73, 83, 85, 91, 137, 139, 141, 153, 155, 165, 167, 197, 205, 223, 237, 247, 253 Patty Orly; 18 Mikhail Zahranichny; 19b, 23t Alfonso de Tomas; 19t Moises Fernandez Acosta; 21t jokihaka; 21c pedrolieb; 22t StockPhotoAstur; 23b Ian Tragen; 24 barbaradudzinska; 25t Baishev; 25b Isantilli; 26t Fotografiche; 26b Janet Faye Hastings; 27t atm2003; 27b OlegD; 28 SOMMAI; 29b mypix; 30t Fedor Kondratenko; 30b l i g h t p o e t; 31 Lilyana Vynogradova; 32b liusimus; 33 Roman Pyshchyk; 34b Chamille White; 34t Timmary; 35t Fotokostic; 35b Pavelk; 36 Apostolos Mastoris; 37b Kuttelvaserova; 37t majaan; 38b, 46 inacio pires; 38t Melpomene; 39t Glenn Price; 40b, 233, 249 Ana del Castillo; 40t Ruggiero Scardigno; 41 photoshut; 42b Diana Taliun; 42t, 43t Dream79; 43b elena moiseeva; 44b stockcreations; 45 Lagui; 49 & 227 WHITE RABBIT83; 50 & 149, 121, 175 Martin Turzak; 53 & 63 Dulce Rubia; 57 mipstudio; 59, 201 bonchan; 75, 119 Brian Maudsley; 81, 99, 101, 185, 209, 213, 225, 229 aguilarphoto; 87 Tobik; 95 Javier Tuana; 103 125, 145, 173, 219, 245 Fernando Sanchez Cortes; 107 fotoedu; 109, 211 Alvaro German Vilela; 111 F.C.G.; 123, 133 Ramon dolarea; 135 cpg-photo; 151 MIMMOHE; 157 Daniel Korzeniewski; 161 Richard M Lee; 163 Joe Gough; 179 Josep M Penalver Rufas; 191 holbox; 195 vesna cvorovic; 199 Charlotte Lake; 203 frescomovie; 215, 241 ampFotoStudio; 235 KarSol; 239 Dimitar Petarchev.

Simple Home Cooking

Tapas

**FLAME TREE
PUBLISHING**

Contents

Ingredients

Equipment

Spanish food has gone quickly from being relatively unknown to being a star on the international food stage. You can find tapas in hip neighbourhoods from New York to London, while in Spain food has reinvented itself. Happily, you can also still find simple tapas in almost any neighbourhood bar. In this book you will find all the classic dishes as well as a few special and delicious recipes that are more unusual.

Introducing Tapas

The word 'tapa' means 'lid' in Spanish and is derived from the verb '*tapar*' which means 'to cover'. There are numerous speculations on how tapas originated. Some people think that it was workers in the fields taking a small meal, such as bread, cheese and olives with them to eat as a snack or while they worked; while others believe the legend about the Castilian King Alfonso the Wise issuing a royal decree saying that everyone should have tapas-style food with their drinks to avoid fighting. Another belief is that it is an old tradition of placing a plate over the customer's drink, usually a glass of wine, to keep out the flies. Over time, the innkeepers realised that if they placed a small, salty snack on the plate the customers would drink more, and so tapas were born. Tapa has evolved through Spain's history as it includes ingredients and influences from other cultures. For example, the Romans invaded Spain and brought with them olives, while the North African Moors brought almonds, oranges and lemons and spices. When the New World was discovered tomatoes, peppers, corn and potatoes were brought back and became quickly integrated into part of the Spanish cuisine as they could be grown in the climate.

What are Tapas?

Today, tapas refer to small dishes or portions of savoury food that can either be cold or hot and eaten as a snack or as a full meal. Tapas may consist of simple bowls of olives or almonds, platters of various Spanish cheeses and meats, or more elaborate warm dishes of meatballs, fried baby squid and snails. Tapas are often placed on pieces of crusty bread, which are called montados or montaditos, and are very common and popular in tapas bars.

There are also pinchos or pintxos (the Basque word), which are tapas with a fine toothpick or cocktail stick through them, and are designed to keep the food from falling off the bread and also to keep track of the number of tapas the customer has eaten. Another name for these is banderilla, as some of them resemble the colourful spears used in bullfighting. These are more common in the Basque country in the north, La Rioja, Asturias and Cantabria. In other areas, namely Madrid, Castilla-La Mancha, Castilla y Leon, Extramadura and in parts of Andalucia, a tapa will be free with your drink, and in several large cities entire areas are dedicated just to tapas bars with each one serving its own unique dish. Throughout Spain there are many tapas competitions with a national 'pinchos and tapas' contest occurring in the city of Valladolid, in Castilla y Leon, every year in November. Over 60 chefs compete to become the best in Spain.

Tapas can be upgraded to bigger portions, which are called raciones. They are generally shared between the diners, and are similar to a Middle Eastern mezze.

Eating Tapas at Home

Eating tapas has become increasingly popular and with a little forward planning it is easy to serve delicious tapas at home for friends and family, with little or no cooking. Tapas are ideal for get-togethers because they are simple to prepare and offer a delicious array of finger foods that your guests can enjoy without getting overfull.

Major supermarkets and high-quality delis now offer lots of Spanish ingredients, such as chorizo, Serrano ham, good-quality olive oil and great Spanish wine, as well as ready-made delicacies. Be sure to use the freshest possible ingredients and try to use what's in season.

When planning your tapas party, focus on creating five or six tapas dishes that aren't too complicated and can be prepared ahead of time. Make sure you have a mix of hot and cold dishes and plan eight pieces per person for a casual drinks party or about 12 pieces per guest if you are planning a tapas dinner. A sample menu could include:

- ❧ Chilli grilled prawns

- ❧ Pan amb tomàquet (Catalan bread with tomatoes)

- ❧ Patatas bravas

- ❧ Classic tortilla

- ❧ Albondigas (meatballs in tomato sauce)

- ❧ Monataditos with goat's cheese, tomato and Padron pepper

In addition, consider the following for your tapas party:

- Meat plays an important role in Spanish cuisine, especially cured meats including Serrano ham, so provide a platter of a selection of cured meats and sausages.

- Spain is also particularly renowned for its goat's and sheep cheese, so purchase Manchego cheese, cut it into cubes and serve on a platter with some delicious quince jelly or membrillo (quince paste).

- A selection of cured olives, fruit, such as figs and slices of melon, dried apricots and stoned dates, roasted, salted almonds and roasted or pickled vegetables and olives are delicious party snacks. Try to find Spanish manzanilla olives and ones stuffed with pimentos and anchovies.

- Every tapas meal has to have bread, so try to buy good-quality crusty fresh bread on the day.

Once you have all the ingredients, it is time to put it all together. Arrange all your tapas in brightly coloured attractive bowls, or in traditional terracotta serving bowls if you have them, together with serving forks, spoons, plenty of napkins and individual serving plates. It is always useful to provide empty bowls for discarded olive stones and cocktail sticks.

No tapas party is complete without drinks, so offer some Spanish wine such as a chilled Cava, a jug of ice-cold Sangria or even a glass of sherry.

Introducing Tapas

Food Culture in Spain

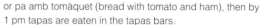

In Spain, the meals and nibbles are spread out throughout the day. Eating is very important to Spaniards as it's a chance to socialise with friends. To start the day, a simple breakfast consisting of strong coffee with hot frothy milk, sweet rolls or toast with jam or a mild cheese is eaten around 8 or 9 am. Many people eat in their local bar as it's a chance to gossip and catch up on the morning papers. By mid-morning, a quick snack is consumed, such as an empanada, or pa amb tomàquet (bread with tomato and ham), then by 1 pm tapas are eaten in the tapas bars.

Lunch starts at around 2 pm and is the largest meal of the day, and it usually consists of a few courses. Local restaurants offer a three-course set meal or menu del dia at very good prices. It usually consists of a starter, then a fish, meat or chicken dish, followed by a dessert. Traditionally, Spaniards have two or three hours for lunch, then take a siesta in the afternoon, but this is becoming rare.

In the late afternoon, at around 5–7 pm, a snack is eaten. This is something simple like a piece of bread with chorizo or salami, then by 8 pm, many people finish work with a drink and a couple of tapas dishes. Dinner is usually eaten late in Spain, often between 9 pm and midnight. This meal is much smaller than lunch; at home it may be an omelette followed by fish and fruit, but dinner in a restaurant is usually larger. During the weekends, Spaniards will socialise and on the way home will stop off at the churros stand to eat these with a hot chocolate. Churros are fried pastries served hot and sprinkled with sugar.

Shopping and Markets

Most Spaniards spend quite a lot of their time and money on food shopping, whether it's in shops or in the local street market – it's a way of life. In the town centres, there are still many independent shops such as greengrocers, butchers and cake shops selling local speciality cakes and pastries as well as confections for the many saints' days and fiestas.

If one of the highlights of Spain is its cuisine, then what better way to see their food than in a typical Spanish market? There are numerous street markets in the towns of Spain and one can be found nearly every day of the week. They can be either daily or weekly. These markets cater for a wide range of goods, from fresh meat, seafood, vegetables and fruit of the particular region to plants, flowers, clothes and bric-a-brac. Shopping at a traditional Spanish market is a cultural experience, as they are bright, gaudy, buzzing with activity and usually very loud. They can either be outdoor street markets, where they take over entire blocks, or indoor covered markets. These weekly street markets are the social highlight of the town and all the cafés and bars are packed full of shoppers. There are a mix of traders who visit each market selling their wares and locals selling fresh seasonal vegetables, eggs and wild mushrooms. You can find some good bargains if you haggle.

Shops and markets don't often open until about 10 am, then they shut at 1 or 2 pm for lunch, then by 5 pm all the shops are open again until about 8 pm.

One of the best-known indoor markets is the Boquéria market in Barcelona, where the best products from the region of Catalonia are sold. This market dates back from 1217, when tables were

set up near the old door of the city to sell meat, then from 1470, a market selling pigs formed. The city authorities decided to set up a separate market consisting of mainly fishmongers and butchers, but it wasn't until 1826 that the market became officially recognised and construction began in 1840 to build a permanent structure. It officially opened in the same year and by 1853 the official inauguration of the structure was made. In 1914 the metal roof was built, which still exists today.

Valencia has a long history of markets, as its people are very proud of their craft and artisan traditions and pottery is very important in the area. Valencia boasts two large food markets, the Mercado Central right in the heart of the city and the Mercado de Colon. The Mercado Central is one of the oldest running food markets in Europe and is well worth visiting. The structure was built of iron in 1928 with high ceilings and a façade beautifully decorated with ceramic tiles and glass – a typical Valencian Modernista style. Restored in 2004, it is a snapshot of Valencian life and offers authentic Valencian produce – you can buy all types of ingredients, such as fresh seafood and meat as well as rare Valencian delicacies. The Mercado de Colon was designed and built by the architect Francisco Mora Berenguer between 1914–16. It is one of the most emblematic Modernist buildings in Valencia and has a colourful façade reminiscent of Gaudí. Inside the building, it is as lively and bustling as any other market. When it first opened the market sold everything from fish to meat, flowers and fruit, but today it is more of a luxury shopping mall with designer shops, a café and a fishmonger with the central area being reserved for cultural events. Outside, tapas bars and boutique shops surround the market.

Equipment

Y̲ou won't need too much specialist equipment to cook authentic tapas dishes, but there are a few pieces that most Spaniards can't live without.

Cazuela

This is the most popular and useful piece of equipment in the Spanish kitchen and every kitchen will have lots of them stacked up waiting to be used. Made from terracotta, the cazuela comes in a range of different sizes and so has lots of different uses, such as a cooking vessel and as an ideal serving dish for tapas. As these dishes are made from clay and are glazed on one side for the food, with an unglazed bottom, they are very fragile. Before using them for cooking they need to be cured, otherwise they will crack.

To cure your cazuela or other terracotta cooking pan before using it for the first time, soak the dish in water for 2 hours for small dishes and 12 hours for larger ones, then drain and dry with a clean tea towel. Fill the dish with water, then put it over a low heat or in a hot oven for 10 minutes. Remove from the heat and leave to cool slowly. After it has cooled down, wash it, then your cazuela is ready for use.

Cazuelas are perfect for cooking indoors over a gas flame or in the oven, or outdoors on the barbecue. It is also recommended when using earthenware pans for cooking to put the meat, fish, chicken and vegetables into the pan before putting it on the heat, to avoid the shock of cold ingredients being put onto the hot clay. After using your cazuela, wash in soapy water, scrubbing with a soft brush to remove any bits of food.

You can buy cazuelas all over Spain, and they are available in specialist kitchen shops and online.

Paella Pan

Paella is the classic Spanish dish and throughout Spain mini paella pans are used for serving substantial tapas such as croquetas or smaller, simpler snacks, such as olives or almonds.

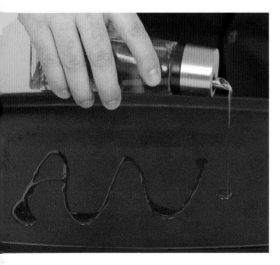

Griddle Pan

Griddle pans are perfect for grilling slices of aubergine, courgettes, pieces of fruit and prawns. When using a griddle pan, make sure to preheat it before adding the food. If you don't have a griddle pan, then a cast-iron frying pan can be used.

Frying Pans

In Spain terracotta frying pans are also used. They are similar to cazuelas, but have a hollow, moulded handle, so it doesn't get too hot to touch and allows it to be moved easily on the hob or barbecue. They are also perfect for serving tapas at the table. Before using an earthenware frying pan, it will need to be

cured (*see* cazuelas above).
Alternatively, use a cast-iron frying
pan or a nonstick one.

Pestle and Mortar

This is another piece of equipment
that is extremely useful in the Spanish
kitchen. Traditionally, it was used for
crushing garlic and herbs, grinding
nuts and for making sauces, such as
the classic allioli (*see* page 86) and
romesco sauce to accompany calcots
(*see* page 186).

Pestles and mortars are available in
hardwood, ceramic or stone, and
come in many different sizes, but a
heavy-duty granite one with a bowl of
about 15 cm/6 inches in diameter is
the best one to use. You can buy
pestles and mortars in any kitchen
shop or online.

Pintxo Sticks

These are flat-shaped toothpicks and are perfect for making pintxos (or food on a stick), as the
flat face holds the food better than ordinary thin cocktail sticks or toothpicks. They are available
in different sizes and can be bought from specialist kitchen shops or online. Cocktail sticks can
be used instead.

Equipment

Spanish Produce

❧

Spanish cuisine is simple, down-to-earth food. It is based on locally sourced and regionally grown fresh ingredients, from fresh aubergines, onions, tomatoes and lemons to cheeses, cured hams and bacon and fish just caught by the local fishermen. Olive oil and garlic are very common ingredients in Spanish food, as are wine and sherry, and every region has its own distinct specialities.

Spanish ingredients are increasingly available in the UK, and major supermarkets and delis now stock a whole variety of olive oil, olives, chorizo, Serrano ham and sherry vinegar, as well as saffron and pimentón, which is used a lot in Spanish cooking. To make the most of preparing tapas, try to find all the ingredients in the following pages and keep them in stock so you can quickly prepare delicious tapas when you have guests coming round for drinks or dinner. If you don't have the same ingredients or can't find a specific ingredient, you can easily substitute with something similar.

Cured Meats and Sausages

The Spanish charcuterie board can be made from a selection of many cured meats. There are many to choose from, such as Serrano ham, Iberico ham, Fuet and Chorizo. Butifarra, which are sausages from Catalonia, or Morcilla, a type of black pudding, are for cooking, as are some chorizos. It is quite normal when enjoying some tapas dishes that a platter of meats is served, piled on bread and topped with pickled peppers or other pickles. The meat is then finished off with a drizzle of Spanish extra virgin olive oil, often skewered with cocktail sticks and accompanied by a small glass of beer.

～ Iberico Ham – This ham is reputed to be one of the most expensive and superior hams made in Spain. It is made from the hocks of pigs and has only recently begun to be exported. The ham's robust flavour is due to the meat being streaked with a sweet, nutty fat, probably due to the pigs' diet of just acorns combined with a moderate amount of exercise roaming through the woods, living a totally free-range lifestyle on the borders between Portugal and Spain.

～ Serrano Ham – Most Serrano hams are made from the Landrace breed of white pigs and are not thought as highly of as Iberico ham; nevertheless, Serrano ham is delicious to eat and is often used as a substitute for its more expensive cousin. The preparation of the ham is important to the quality of the finished meat. First of all, once the hams are ready to be prepared, they are trimmed and cleaned, before being stacked and covered with salt. They are then left for at least two weeks. This is done in order to draw off the excess moisture and prevent the meat from spoiling. The salt is then washed off and the hams are hung to dry for about six months. Finally, the hams are hung in a cool, dry place for six to eighteen months, depending on the climate, as well as the size and type of ham being cured.

～ Spanish Produce

The drying sheds are usually built at high elevations, which is why the ham is called mountain ham. There are many different types of Spanish ham, but there are a few guidelines on how to judge which hams are the best quality. Perhaps the two most important factors are the type of pig used and its lifestyle and diet.

❧ Cecina – This is a salt-cured, air-dried beef, and is truly a delicacy of Spain. The origin of the name 'cecina' is not altogether clear. Some believe that it comes from Latin 'siccus', meaning 'dry', while others believe it originates from the Celtic word 'cieroina' which refers to the north wind that blows across Spain. It is produced in the same way as it was hundreds of years ago. For centuries, homes in the Maragara area (in the northwest of Spain) traditionally kept a dried beef leg in the larder to feed the family.

❧ Pork Loin – Pork and wild boar play a very important part in Spanish cuisine, whether fresh or cured. A cured loin is called 'lonzino' and is normally dry-cured, which becomes pink in colour as it ages and slices very easily. The taste is similar to ham and it is reputed to be almost as good as prosciutto.

❧ Chorizo – There are two types of chorizo: fresh, which will need cooking before eating, and a cured smoked sausage, which can be eaten straight away. Generally, the cured chorizo is used and is a popular ingredient in the tapas menu, where it is usually sliced and eaten. Evidently chorizo plays an important part in Spanish cuisine. It is perhaps the best-known of the Spanish sausages (a slightly different chorizo can also be found in Mexico). There are many varieties of

Spanish sausages that are cured through air-drying before they are ready to be eaten. Chorizo is a mixture of pork fat, lean pork meat, pimento (smoked paprika) and garlic. It is this pimento that gives the chorizo its red colour as well as its spicy, smoky flavour. Pimentón can be sweet, bittersweet or hot.

❧ Fuet – This is a Catalan dry-cured sausage made from pork and is extremely versatile in its use. It can be added to a variety of dishes, eaten on bread, or often it is served on a chopping board on the dinner table. It is perhaps best eaten when served in this traditional manner.

❧ Longaniza – This sausage is very similar to chorizo, with the main difference being that black pepper is used instead of paprika.

❧ Sobrasada – Sobrasada is a traditional pork sausage from Mallorca, flavoured with paprika, salt and black pepper. It is encased in skins and matured slowly using traditional methods.

❧ Botifarra – This sausage comes in either white or black from the Catalonian region of Spain. The white sausage is made from pork, tripe and pine nuts, while the black sausage is made from blood, belly of pork and spices.

❧ Morcilla – This sausage uses fillings such as rice or onions as its main ingredient, but it can also contain pig's blood or pork fat.

Cheese

Cheese plays a very important part in Spanish cuisine. Unfortunately, some of the cheeses are rarely heard of outside Spain, which is a pity. Here, we are talking about just a small selection of five very distinct and more readily available cheeses, all of which have their own characteristics and are well worth looking out for.

❧ Cabrales – This cheese is still made traditionally by artisans in the north of Spain. It is made from unpasturised cows' milk and retains the flavour from the meadows where the cows graze. It can also be a blended cheese using both sheep's milk and goats' milk giving a much stronger flavour.

The milk used to make this cheese comes only from one region, Asturias. To make the cheese, the milk first has to be heated before rennet is added to make the milk curdle. The whey is skimmed off and discarded. The remaining curds are packed into a mould and salted, then left for about two weeks. The cheese is then allowed to age for a further two to five months in limestone caves in the mountains. After this, the cheese is placed on wooden racks and turned occasionally and cleaned at the same time. This produces a cheese that has blue/greenish veins running through it, with a distinctive and strong flavour. The cheese, made from a blend of milks, has a far stronger flavour than cheese made just from cows' milk.

❧ Mahón – This white cheese, made from cow's milk, varies from being soft to hard. The name comes from the port of Mahón on the Spanish island of Minorca. Again, this cheese has some very distinct characteristics, some of which are due to ageing. This cheese has a wonderfully smooth, buttery flavour, which is slightly acidic and salty, as well as an aroma which is nutty with a hint of fruity sweetness when eating. This is due to the sea salt in the grass, which the cows graze on. Generally the rind is orange in colour, as it is rubbed with butter or oil and paprika while the cheese is maturing, which takes about ten months. During this time, small holes develop in the cheese, which is one of its characteristics.

∾ Manchego – This cheese is made in the Spanish region of La Mancha using milk from La Manchega breed of sheep. The cheese is normally aged from between three months to two years. It has a firm and compact texture with a buttery flavour and often contains small air pockets which are the little holes seen throughout the cheese. The colour of the cheese varies from white to ivory-yellow, and the inedible rind from yellow to brownish beige. On maturity, the cheese has a distinctive flavour, well developed but not too strong, creamy with a slight piquancy, and leaves an aftertaste that is characteristic of sheep's milk. Manchego is quite widely available in the UK.

∾ Tetilla – This cheese is sometimes referred to as 'perilla', has been made in Galicia since 1993 and is the fourth most important Spanish cheese made in the region. Authentic tetilla cheese always comes with its origins clearly displayed and a certificate of origin. Nowadays it is produced throughout the Galician region, using milk from

Spanish Produce

the Galician blonde cows. However, it used to be produced in small towns and villages along its borders. The name 'tetilla' means 'small breast', which describes the shape of the cheese. It has a cone topping which has a 'nipple' at the very top, or a half pear, hence its other name, 'perilla' cheese. It weighs between ½ and 1½ kg, with a diameter and height ranging from 9 to 15 cm. It is used as a dessert cheese as well as in savoury cooking.

∾ Murcia al Vino – This cheese is from the Murcia region in southeastern Spain. It is made from the milk of goats and is unusual in that it is bathed in wine during the production process, giving the rind its distinctive red wine colour and the cheese its aroma. The cheese is slightly salty in taste. In the UK, this cheese is often referred to as Drunken Goat, and is increasingly available in supermarkets.

Fresh Meat

∾ Pork – Pork is perhaps the most popular meat in Spain and there are many recipes using all manner of pork cuts in Spanish cuisine. Whether the pork is fresh or cured, the Spanish have a recipe or two for that particular cut of meat. Nothing is wasted, from trotters to brain – it is all consumed with much gusto and relish. Try any Spanish butcher's shop or 'carniceria' and you will not be disappointed as you will find beautifully displayed cuts of pork presented in many different ways. However, you will not find all of the cuts that you would expect to find in the UK, as they, like other countries, have their own particular cuts, which are typical to each region. The cuts that can be found in Spain consist of loin, ribs, fillet, shoulder, chops and steaks, ground or minced pork, neck and trotters. That is not forgetting the large range of bacon, ham and sausages. The range of pork cuts available in Spanish villages is dictated by the different eating habits. In some areas, such as Andalucia, they cut pork tenderloin lengthways, then open it out flat, and it has been done like this for generations. Pigs' trotters are very popular and can be found for sale daily, ready to be boiled or cooked for a tasty lunch.

❧ Lamb – Lamb and sometimes mutton are available in Spain, but it is not nearly as popular as pork. When shopping for lamb in Spain, it is instantly noticeable that the cuts vary quite considerably from the cuts in the UK. Homegrown lamb often comes from Teruel in the Aragon region where it is often very cold, but luckily there are plenty of woods where the lambs can shelter. The sheep feed on aromatic herbs and produce very fragrant milk, which the young lambs feed on, thus making the flesh extremely fragrant. Lamb in this region is absolutely delicious and a must when travelling through or staying for a few days. The chief cuts of lamb in Spain are: lamb chops (chuletas de cordero), leg of lamb (pierna de cordero), shoulder of lamb (paletilla de cordero), lamb mince (carne picada de cordero) and stewing lamb (guisado de cordero). It is useful to know what you are shopping for when entering a Spanish butcher's shop or supermarket, and which cut of lamb you are ordering in a restaurant; that way you are more likely to enjoy Spanish lamb at its best.

❧ Tripe – Although tripe is no longer popular in the UK, that is not so in Spain and many other countries. The French are particularly fond of tripe (andouille) and it is served in high-class restaurants as well as country-style restaurants or cafés. Tripe can also be served in Italy, Morocco and many countries in Eastern Europe. Tripe is presented in many different ways, from grilled to stewed.

It needs careful preparation but is an economical and nutritious meal. Tripe can come from all farm animals, beef, pork and lamb and is the lining of the stomach.

To prepare tripe, first of all make sure that the tripe has been 'washed' (this is normally done by a professional person well used to the task) and is not 'green' as tripe that has not been washed before selling is considered unfit to eat. Washed tripe is normally referred to as 'dressed tripe'. The tripe is boiled gently with various herbs and seasoning for 2–2 ½ hours, which bleaches it, and it becomes paler and sort of creamy white in colour. After boiling it can be coated in a sauce then cooked again for about 45 minutes before serving.

Chicken – Chicken is perhaps the most universally popular meat of all. There are many reasons for this: chicken is highly nutritious and, after the skin is discarded, it contains little fat and is an excellent source of protein. In Spain most of the chicken is used. Perhaps the only parts that are not eaten are the feet and head. The giblets are used for stock.

There are a few different types of chicken produced both in Spain and the rest of the world. These range from the baby or spring chicken, which is tiny and sufficient for one portion; slightly larger is the poussin; then the roasting chicken, which is normally around 1.5 kg/3 lb in weight; the capon is the largest chicken available. It is similar to a small turkey, and is usually available around Christmas.

The Spanish cuts of chicken are very similar to the UK and the rest of the world. In Spanish cuisine, chicken is used in numerous dishes, including casseroles and stews containing butter and haricot beans and lentils.

Seafood

- Cuttlefish – These belong to the cephalopoda family and, despite their name, cuttlefish are not fish but molluscs. They taste delicious and are similar to squid and octopus, to which they are related. Cuttlefish have a large head and small tentacles. They also have an exceptionally bony frame, which contains copious amounts of black ink. This leads to them being fished heavily for their ink to be used in pasta and risotto. They generally range in size from 15 cm/6 inches to 25 cm/ 10 inches, and over 10.5 kg/23 lb in weight. They eat small fish and shellfish, such as whitebait, octopus and crabs. Cuttlefish are normally cleaned when frozen, but if this hasn't been done, then ask your fishmonger to do this. If you would like to do this yourself, clean them in the same manner as cleaning squid. They are cooked either in rapidly boiling water for 2–3 minutes or gently stewed for about 2 hours. They can also be fried on a griddle pan for a few minutes before eating.

- Shrimps – Shrimps or prawns come in various sizes. Only the smallest are known as shrimp in the UK, while in nearly all other countries all shrimps or prawns are known as shrimp. They come from the crustaceans family and can be found worldwide either fresh or frozen, peeled or left with their shells, heads and

Spanish Produce

tentacles intact. They are grey in colour when raw, but after cooking both the flesh and shells turn pink. Under no circumstances should they be eaten raw or if they have a nasty smell, as they may give you a very nasty tummy problem. Fresh shrimps/prawns should smell of the sea and cooked ones should not smell too much, with only a faint smell of the sea. They are very easy to prepare. Raw prawns can be cooked with or without their heads and shells on. Simply rinse then grill, pan-fry or cook in boiling water for 3–5 minutes until the shells are pink. Either serve (with finger bowls to rinse the fingers) immediately, or cool, then discard the heads, shells and legs and serve. There are many delicious recipes for shrimps/prawns in Spain and throughout the world.

∽ Squid – Squid comes from the same family as cuttlefish and is found in the same environment and habitat. With more people travelling to most parts of the world, there are some fish and seafood that have grown in popularity and squid is one of these. Squid can be prepared very easily. Pull the tentacles away from the squid body and feel inside for the quill. Pull it out and discard. Rinse well, then remove the ears (wing-like flaps) and the purplish skin, leaving only the white meat. Cut off the tentacles and remove and discard the hard beak. Slice the squid body into rings, or cut down one side, and clean thoroughly. Score the inside lightly in a cross-hatch pattern. Cook as per the recipe. If making squid rings, cut into rings, dip into seasoned flour and pan-fry for 2–3 minutes. It is vital that squid is not overcooked, otherwise it can become very tough and almost inedible. Squid rings can also be dropped into a light batter, then deep-fried; the name for this dish in Spain is calamares.

∽ Clams – Clams are bivalve molluscs and there are over 2,000 varieties. They are either hard- or soft-shelled and come in various sizes; some are too small to worry about for culinary purposes. Many clams have a roughly oval shape; however, the edible Pacific razor clam has an elongated, parallel-sided shell and look like an old-fashioned razor. As soon as you buy them, place either in cold water to cover and leave in a cool place or wrap tightly and store in the refrigerator. It is advisable to prepare them just before eating. Scrub the clam shells with a soft brush and remove any barnacles. Discard any clams that are open and do not close when tapped lightly on the work surface. Have ready a very large saucepan with a lid, in which you have made the cooking liquor. When boiling, lower the cleaned clams into the boiling liquid and cover with the lid. Cook for 5–7 minutes, stirring occasionally, until the clams have opened. Discard any clams that are closed, and serve. This is a classic way of cooking clams; however there are many other delicious recipes to try, some of which are included in this book.

❧ Mussels – Mussels used to be very popular in bygone years and were considered to be a good cheap food that was full of protein, and were readily eaten by the working class. However, over the years their popularity waned and they fell out of fashion. But fashion changes and now they, like oysters, are held in high regard by food 'buffs' and gourmets. The UK is still slightly hesitant about eating mussels, but they are enjoyed with gusto in Spain and other European countries. Mussels should be prepared in exactly the same way as clams. Mussels used to be seasonal when they were only caught in the wild, but are now also farmed. In Spain they provide a delicious meal often served just as they are with bread and chips.

Spanish Produce

❧ Crab – Crabs are crustaceans and are fished around the world. They are still considered to be a bit of a luxury, probably due to the fact that they are hard to fish and to prepare. If you are lucky enough to have a good fishmonger or live by the sea, you will most probably find they are readily available. Canned crab meat in brine, or frozen crab meat, is available, but the flavour is not as good as a fresh crab. Unless you buy your crab straight from the fisherman, in most cases it will be sold cooked and dressed ready for eating. If so, enjoy! Most crabs have a hard shell, although there are soft-shelled crabs in the USA and in other parts of the world. Many crabs live both in the water and on land, especially in tropical climates.

❧ Anchovies – Anchovies can be bought both fresh and canned in oil or brine. They are small fish which can be found in many oceans of the world, and are a great favourite in Spain. If eating fresh, the fish should be eaten as soon as possible after catching. Wash the fish well, then dry and dip in seasoned flour. Fry in batches in a deep-fryer basket, for 3–4 minutes until golden, then drain and serve with bread and lemon wedges to squeeze over. The fish are eaten whole: head, tail and body. Anchovies are small and bony and often bought already salted as a method of preservation. The anchovy salting tradition, as with other fish, dates back to ancient times when places such as Santoña (Cantabria) and other towns along the Basque coast continued to carry out this tradition until almost the end of the 19th century. Preparing the fish for canning is a skill that has been handed down through the generations. First, the fish are salted and left to cure for several months before being packed in small cans or jars. Next, if the fish are to be packed in brine, the heads are washed, then placed in the containers which are topped up with salt and sealed. If packed in oil, the fish are skinned, washed, trimmed to size, then dried and filleted. Finally, they are placed in containers and covered with olive oil before sealing.

❧ Fresh and Canned Tuna – Tuna can be bought either fresh or canned. Canned tuna is extremely popular, can be found worldwide and is inexpensive to buy; whereas fresh tuna is not that readily available and, unlike canned, is quite difficult to find and is expensive to buy in the UK. Tuna belongs to the same group of fish as mackerel and bonito. There are a few varieties of tuna, which vary greatly in size, from the bullet tuna which is about 50 cm/1.6 ft, to the Atlantic blue fin tuna which is 458 cm/15 ft in length. It has been known that the blue fin tuna can live for up to 50 years if it does not get caught. Another variety of tuna is yellow fin tuna, which is extremely fast, reaching speeds of up to 75 km per hour.

Vegetables

❧ Olives – Olives play an important part in Spanish cuisine, as they are used in the making of olive oil, and the whole olive is used in many dishes either as an integral part of the recipe or as a garnish. Olives are grown throughout the Mediterranean and vast olive groves can be found in Spain, where the hot and sunny climate is ideal for growing them. These olive groves are owned by families who either process their olives themselves, or sell them to larger owners

or corporations. Those families who have owned the groves over generations are often forced to sell to the corporations as it is no longer financially viable to process the olives themselves. Olives are either green or black and are sold ready prepared. Some are pitted and left whole, others are pitted and stuffed with red pimento, or a large blanched almond, anchovy fillet or garlic, then packed in jars or cans and covered with oil, brine or a spicy oil which marinates the olives before they are eaten.

∾ Piquillo Peppers – These little peppers are a variety of a chilli pepper but unlike a chilli pepper do not carry quite a kick when eating. They are more like their bigger cousin the bell pepper. They are grown extensively in the north of Spain near the town of Lodosa and their name translates into 'little beak'. They are not generally exported as they are so popular that the Spanish like to keep them for themselves. They are hand picked twice a year, from September to December, once they have soaked up the hot sun and grown as large as they can, and are left whole. They are then roasted over a dying fire so that they are exposed to the embers of the fire which help to increase the spicy flavour. This roasting also helps to increase the hint of sweetness. Once the peppers have cooled after the roasting, they are left whole and peeled and packed into cans or jars. Piquillo peppers are used for the decoration of many traditional dishes and on top of many tapas snacks. They can also be found stuffed with cheese, meat or fish, again served as an appetizer or in a selection of tapas dishes.

∾ Artichokes – Artichokes or, as we call them, globe artichokes, are extremely popular in Spain and are used in many traditional spanish dishes. The artichoke is a vegetable that belongs to the same family as lettuce and endive. It is a perennial thistle and can grow from 4–6 feet in height with large silver-green leaves. Years ago the artichoke was thought to be an aphrodisiac and women were not allowed to eat them! Fortunately, that myth is no longer believed. The artichoke originally came from North Africa and is still grown in countries around the Mediterranean. Spain is one of the largest growers of artichokes, both for the home market and for export. There are a few varieties grown including the Blanca de Tudela, which varies slightly in size, colour and shape but still retains its overall properties of the artichoke. Artichokes are grown quite easily in the UK and are normally ready in early summer. There is a recipe in this book which describes how they should be prepared and cooked, *see* page 204. The heart of the artichoke is eaten – the leaves are simply pulled off the cooked vegetable and dipped into a sauce such as allioli and then sucked. It is also possible to buy artichoke hearts in cans or in jars.

∾ Mushrooms – There are many different mushrooms, both wild and cultivated, providing a very useful and delicious ingredient. When gathering wild mushrooms take great care as not all wild mushrooms are edible and in fact some are poisonous and could be fatal. So if foraging, always take a comprehensive book or better still a mushroom expert when gathering these delights. However, it is possible to buy dried or fresh wild mushrooms. If using dried ones, simply cover in warm water for at least 10 minutes, then drain and use. Strain the soaking liquid before using. Before using fresh wild mushrooms, trim the stalks and then either gently brush or wipe the mushroom cap with kitchen paper to remove any dirt. Thee are a few types of cultivated mushrooms available. Button mushrooms are tiny white mushrooms that are left whole, while closed cup are larger versions of the button and are normally trimmed at the end of the stalk, left whole or cut into slices or quarters. Then there are some mushrooms that are the same as the other two

∾   Spanish Produce

but much larger, and these are normally stuffed or chopped. Field mushrooms are large, quite flat mushrooms and suitable for stuffing. With these mushrooms it is sometimes advisable to peel the skin. Chestnut mushrooms are almost the same as the closed cup but with a brown skin. Mushrooms have a porous skin and should not be washed at all, simply wipe clean with absorbent kitchen paper just before use.

❧ Garlic – Garlic can be found both as wild garlic or as a garlic bulb and is delicious. It adds flavour to any dish it is cooked in. However, it has to be said that some people do not like garlic or are allergic to it. Look for wild garlic in woods and sometimes in hedgerows. Wild garlic is very similar in appearance to spring onions and should be trimmed in the same manner. They are quite strong so if eating raw, do so sparingly. Use as normal if cooking with them. Whole garlic bulbs are grown the world over and play a very important part in all cuisines. It is also possible to obtain smoked garlic, which as its name suggests has a smoky aroma and taste, which is quite subtle. When using garlic it is often a question of personal taste how you prepare the garlic. Normally the bulb is broken into cloves, which are peeled. You can either slice, chop or crush the bulb according to preference. Each method slightly alters the taste of the garlic. Crushing garlic is best for stuffings and dishes that are not cooked for a long time; chopping is ideal for pan-frying; while slicing is good for roasting and dishes that need longer to cook.

❧ Onions – Spain is famous for its beautiful Spanish onion, which is round with yellow or white flesh and very large with a mild, sweetish flavour. It is exported to the UK and the rest of Europe and is highly valued for cooking.

It is ideal for stuffing as well as for all other recipes that use onion. Because of its mild, sweet flavour it is often eaten raw. Coming from the *Allium cepa* plant family, a Spanish onion is quite similar to a red onion and is only slightly different in taste, though noticeably different in appearance.

∾ Tomatoes – Coming in a variety of different shapes, sizes and colours, tomatoes are universally loved. The tomatoes that Spain grows are ripe and bursting with flavour due to their climate. They feature heavily in both raw and cooked dishes, whether it is as tiny cherry tomatoes which are so sweet they can be eaten like sweets or the larger variety of cherry tomatoes that are now available in red, orange or yellow. You can also now buy cherry plum tomatoes that are used so often in pasta dishes, or Beefsteak tomatoes which are extremely large and ideal for stuffing. There are also several byproducts which also add flavour to dishes. These range from passata, which is sieved tomato purée, to tomato ketchup and tubes or small cans of tomato paste or purée. Many of these products use tomatoes grown in hot sunny climates such as Spain so that they get all the flavour possible.

∾ Aubergine – Aubergine, or as it is called in many countries, eggplant, originally came from India and Asia and surrounding areas, but is now grown in other countries as well, including Spain. There are various varieties available, including a white aubergine and one that has pale purple and white stripes down its length. It is important to know how to treat aubergines, especially large ones that have a tendency to be bitter. To counteract this, it is advisable to rinse first, then slice. Discard the stem at the top. Layer the slices in a

colander in the sink or over a bowl (to catch the drips) with salt and leave for at least 30 minutes or longer. After this, rinse thoroughly and pat dry with absorbent kitchen paper. To cook aubergine slices, fry the slices in olive oil for 10 minutes or so, then turn them over and cook until the they are tender. In these days of watching your diet, a way to cut down the amount of oil used is to brush both sides of the aubergine slices with oil and place under a preheated grill. Cook on both sides for 3–5 minutes until soft, then use.

∾ Red Peppers – Red peppers are one of those ingredients that many people wonder how they ever managed without. These days, red, green, yellow, orange and occasionally black peppers can be seen in the markets or shops. They provide extra flavour as well as a welcome flash of colour in recipes, especially in the winter. They are sometimes called 'sweet peppers' in contrast to their fiery cousins the chilli pepper. Peppers are native to Mexico, Central America and northern South America. Pepper seeds were later carried back to Spain in 1493, and from there spread to other European, African and Asian countries. Today, China is the world's largest pepper producer, followed by Mexico. Peppers can be eaten raw or cooked. If eaten raw they have a crisp, crunchy texture and unlike chilli peppers a mild taste, even if you eat the seeds or membrane which the seeds are attached to. For some dishes, just the pepper flesh is eaten as it is smooth and soft and can easily be puréed for a soup or dip. In these cases you will need to remove the skin first.

∾ Potatoes – It is believed that potatoes were brought back to England from Spain as a present for Elizabeth I. It is also thought, due to ancient records, that the potato originated in Peru.

It quickly became very popular and was adopted by many countries. This was partly due to it being very easy to grow and a cheap source of food. Potatoes are grown the world over and there are many different varieties. They are sold classed as either red- or white-skinned. There are different potatoes for different purposes and are broadly classified into waxy and floury types. New or baby potatoes are available all year round.

Spinach – Spinach is an excellent source of vitamin C but only contains a moderate amount of iron. Spinach should look crisp and full of colour; avoid any that is limp and not bright green. Ideally it should be picked and eaten within an hour, or at least eaten on the same day it is harvested. The leaves need to be thoroughly washed before cooking, using only the water that remains on the leaves after washing. Baby spinach leaves have become very popular recently and are used in salads and as a garnish. These should be harvested and eaten as soon as possible after picking. Spinach is very easy to prepare. Wash the leaves thoroughly and if the white stalk that runs through the centre of each leaf looks tough, then strip the leaves down, discarding the stalk. Place the washed spinach in a large saucepan, and remember that the spinach will greatly reduce when cooked. Add a little salt, place on the hob and cover with the lid. Cook for 3–4 minutes until the spinach has wilted and is reduced in volume by half. Drain and gently press out the excess water and chop lightly.

Spanish Produce

≈ Pumpkins – There are countless different varieties of pumpkins and winter squash, and many of the varieties are grown on UK farms. They are growing in popularity and these days play an important part in many diets. Pumpkins and squashes are used in savoury dishes, as well as desserts and cakes. A pumpkin is a gourd-like squash with a thick, orange, yellow or green shell or rind. This is creased from the stem to the base and contains the seeds and pulp. Pumpkins and other squashes are widely grown both for domestic and commercial use. The numerous varieties of squashes grown these days include acorn, butternut and little gem, a smaller dark green squash. To cook pumpkin and other squashes, cut in halves or quarters and peel. Scoop out the seeds and pulp. Depending on what you are going to do with the flesh: either cut into small pieces and cook in boiling water for about 5 minutes to soften, then place in hot oil and roast; or cook in boiling water until soft, then drain, mash or dice and use according to your recipe. You can also add pumpkin to casseroles and stews.

≈ Lemons – Lemons are used in both savoury and sweet dishes in Spain, varying from casseroles and rice dishes, to flavouring fish dishes, desserts, cakes and biscuits. They are also used in drinks for medicinal purposes as well as in soft or alcoholic drinks. Both the rind or zest can be used, as well as the juice. In some cases, for example, when roasting a chicken, a whole lemon with some fresh herbs is placed in the cavity of the chicken prior to cooking for added flavour. Lemons and, in fact, all citrus fruit need to be grown in hot sunny climates for the best results. Lemons can be found growing in back gardens or on the wayside in Spain, the USA and South of France and Italy as well as in Asia. They do not grow well in the UK.

Beans and Pulses

❧ **Chickpeas** – These are grown in the Mediterranean, western Asia and Australia. If buying dried chickpeas, look for firm ones with a uniform beige colour. Choose canned chickpeas stored in water, rather than brine. Dried chickpeas can be stored in a cool, dark place for up to one year without deterioration. Cooked chickpeas can be frozen. Some varieties of chickpeas can even be popped and eaten like popcorn. If using dried, they need to be soaked in cold water overnight before cooking. This begins the softening process. The next day, drain the chickpeas, place in a saucepan, cover with twice the amount of water and bring to the boil. If liked, flavourings can be added, such as bay leaves, onion and seasoning; then the chickpeas are covered with the lid and simmered for about 2–2½ hours or until tender. They can be used in stews, casseroles, in salads and to make flour.

❧ **Lentils** – These are part of the pulse family and are the edible seed of certain leguminous plants. All types of pulses and beans, including lentils, have been around for thousands of years – even today they play an important part in many people's diets in Europe, the Middle East, the Caribbean and South America. Lentil colours range from yellow to red-orange, green, brown and black. The lentils most readily available and perhaps the most popular are: split red lentils, split yellow lentils, green lentils and Puy lentils, said by many to be the best of all. Most lentils need only a short cooking time: from 10–40 minutes, depending on which variety is used.

Spanish Produce

The small varieties with the husk removed, such as the common split red lentil require about 10 minutes while the Puy lentil takes up to 40 minutes. Lentils are used throughout the Mediterranean regions including Spain and are used in a variety of dishes.

~ Fabes/Habas/ Broad Beans – The term fava bean (from the Italian 'fava', meaning 'broad bean') is usually used in English-speaking countries such as the USA; but the term 'broad bean' is the most common name in the UK. These beans are not as popular in the UK as in other parts of the world. It is possible to buy fresh broad beans, but their growing season is quite short, so look for either canned broad beans or frozen ones. But remember, unlike most produce they are definitely seasonal. Fresh broad beans consist of a long pod which needs shelling, similar to fresh peas; then the beans inside the pod are removed and cooked in lightly salted boiling water for 15–20 minutes, depending on how young they are. Drain and serve with a knob of butter. They can also be used in risottos, rice dishes, casseroles and stews. Broad beans have been cultivated over thousands of years and are among the easiest to grow, together with lentils, peas and chickpeas. They are often grown as a cover crop to prevent erosion of the soil as they can be left over the winter months and leave nitrogen in the soil. In Spain, broad beans are used with many ingredients and flavourings, such as with ham, paprika, preserved lemons, black botifarra sausage and in tortillas.

~ Spanish White Bean – Spanish white beans, similar to haricot or cannelini beans, are small, plump, dry, white beans and have a mild flavour. Like other dried beans, they will keep for a year or more when stored correctly in the cool and dark. Avoid buying beans that are discolored, as they may have been poorly handled while they dried. When using, first rinse them and pick through them to remove small stones and organic material, which may have been packaged with them. These beans, like their counterparts, have to be soaked overnight in plenty of cold water. They are then rinsed and covered with fresh water, with seasoning and flavouring to taste, and brought to the boil. Any scum that rises to the top is skimmed off; then the beans are cooked for 1–1½ hours or until tender. They are then ready for eating. Spanish white beans are available in Spanish shops or on the internet, and it is also possible to buy canned haricot and cannelini beans to use as a substitute. In both cases the beans need rinsing under cold running water before using. White beans play an important part in the Spanish kitchen and are used in stews, casseroles, soups and well known dishes such as Asturian Bean Stew (*see* page 144).

Olive Oil

Olives are grown almost everywhere in Spain, from the mountains in the north to Andalucia in the south, so for centuries, olives and olive oil have been an integral part of Spanish life. Olive oil is an essential part of Spanish cooking and this may be the reason why the Mediterranean diet has been deemed so healthy. There are three main types of olive oil: extra virgin olive oil, which is the most expensive, has a superb flavour and is made by extracting the oil straight from the olive in a process called cold pressing; fine or virgin olive oil, which is also produced by natural methods; and pure olive oil, which is blander and is a blend of either extra virgin or virgin olive oil and olive oil that are refined. Olive oil loses its colour and aroma if it is exposed to light, so always store in a cool dark place.

Spanish Produce

Herbs ❧ Spices

Herbs and spices play an important part in Spanish cooking. When using herbs it is best to use fresh, if possible, as they will give the best flavour. For a full flavour, grind spices whenever possible, rather than using ready ground. Both dried herbs and spices should only be kept for 1–2 months and should be kept in a cool dark place. Exposure to light ruins the flavour. Remember also, that 1 teaspoon of dried herb or spice is the equivalent to 1 tablespoon of fresh.

❧ Rosemary – A hardy plant, which in the right conditions grows into a large bush. It has very spiky leaves which, when lightly crushed or chopped, release an aroma of camphor. It originated from the Mediterranean and is used extensively with meat, especially lamb, and fish. Ground dried rosemary is available, but fresh is more commonly used.

❧ Bay – This plant is also known as sweet bay and is related to the laurel family. It is found extensively in Mediterranean countries. Take care that you get the correct plant if planting, as laurel leaves are poisonous. Normally used fresh, the leaf is rinsed, then added to many dishes, from meat and fish dishes to sauces and puddings. It has a delicate flavour and is one of the main ingredients in a bouquet garni.

❧ Thyme – A very well known and popular herb, thyme originates from the Mediterranean and can be used in most savoury dishes such as casseroles, stews, soups and poultry, which are often stuffed with a thyme stuffing. Thyme is a robust herb in spite of having tiny leaves, and generally it is added at the beginning of cooking. There are other varieties of thyme available and perhaps the best known alternative is a lemon-scented variety, which really does have lemony overtones.

∽ Oregano – Also known as 'wild marjoram', oregano is grown in Asia, as well as around the Mediterranean. It is aromatic, which combines well with tomatoes, eggs, cheese. Use sparingly, for although the leaves are relatively small, they do have quite a powerful taste and aroma.

∽ Marjoram – Grown extensively in the Mediterranean and Asia, this herb is like oregano, and is also known as sweet marjoram. It is used in the same way as oregano and often one herb is substituted for the other.

∽ Parsley – Parsley is another herb that is grown in the Mediterranean. It is possibly the most well known of all herbs. There are a few varieties, but without a doubt the best-known varieties are the curly leaf and the flat-leaf (also known as continental in some countries). It can be used in savoury dishes, in bouquet garni and as a garnish for many dishes either in the form of sprigs or chopped fresh parsley. It can also be chopped and frozen if wished. Parsley stalks especially have a celery taste, which becomes more pungent when chopped.

∽ Saffron – This spice is reputed to be the most expensive spice in the world, with a street value similar to gold. It comes from the stamens of the crocus, will colour food yellow and has a very distinctive taste. Use too much and it turns the dish bitter and in some cases inedible. It takes 75,000 stamens to produce 450 g/ 1 lb of saffron. It is possible to buy saffron in powder form but usually it is available as strands. It is extremely easy to use, simply soak about ¼ teaspoon of saffron strands in about 2–3 tablespoons warm water, and leave for 10–15 minutes to allow the colour to come out. When ready to use, add to the dish with the soaking liquid. It is possible to buy a cheaper version, but it is not a good substitute as the flavour and colour is harsh. Turmeric can also be used as a cheap substitute, but again the colour and taste are vastly inferior.

Herbs & Spices

Pimenton – Chilli powder or pimenton comes from the small red chillies that are grown on the hillside of Spain. They are picked in the autumn and taken to smoke houses nearby. Here they are place in oak casks and smoked for 15 days. The peppers are turned every day. After this the seeds are removed, then the peppers are ground in stone mill. This results in a deep red aromatic spice, which is then used the length and breadth of Spain and is responsible for the deep red colour of Chorizo and other ingredients and dishes.

Cinnamon – Cinnamon is a very aromatic spice with a sweet and delicate flavour. It comes in two forms, either ground cinnamon or cinnamon sticks. It is the inner bark from a number of trees and originally was only grown in Sri Lanka, but it is now grown in South East Asia, Java and Indonesia. Cinnamon is used in just about everything from aromatic curries to relishes and pickles. Casseroles, desserts, cakes and drinks can all benefit from this spice. Ground cinnamon is normally sprinkled into dishes, whereas cinnamon sticks are normally lightly bruised (bashed gently with a rolling pin), which helps to release the aromatic flavour before they are added to the dish. Discard at the end of cooking.

Nutmeg – Nutmeg is the dried seed inside a lacy cover called mace, which is the fruit from an evergreen tree native to South East Asia. Nutmeg is very hard and needs to be freshly grated (on the fine side of the grater).

Wine & Tapas

Vineyards in Spain are found from the mountains in the north down to the hot sun-drenched coasts in the south – the countryside is literally covered with them. This means that wine drinking is a large part of the Spanish culture and food and wine have become intertwined with each other. When visiting a bar for a drink you will be offered something to nibble on too. This can be as simple as a bowl of almonds or olives or a couple of dishes of tapas. Wine accompanies lunch and dinner and a glass is usually included in the set price. Spain produces some great wines from many of its regions and each has its own colour, aroma and taste.

There are four basic types of Spanish wine: tinto – red; rosado –rosé; blanco –white; and cava – sparkling wine. Most wines in Spain are classified under a regulating system called *Denominaciones de Origen* where quality is strictly controlled, so look for D.O. and D.O.C on wine labels – they aren't necessarily the best wine but you won't go wrong if you choose these. The age of the wine will appear on the label too and each region has its own terms, but a general guideline

is that if you see Gran Reserva or Reserva on the label this means that it has a softer, more complex and rounded flavour, as they have been aged for longer than Joven or young wines.

Red Wine

Spain is known for its red wines and there is a huge range to choose from. Perhaps the best known are wines from the Rioja region, in northern Spain, from Ribera del Duero in Castille and Leon, to Priorat in Catalonia. Young reds, available in many regions, tend to be light and fruity, and can make good tapas wines as they go with a wider range of dishes. However a strong cheese or good quality ham is still probably best matched with a good oak-aged Rioja or something similar.

White Wine

White wine from Spain is usually fresh, crisp, lively and well-balanced, so ideal for fruity tapas dishes or grilled seafood. The Rías Baixas region of Galicia in northwestern Spain provides increasingly well known Albariño wines. Look also for Galician wines such as the D.O. Ribeiro, Ribeira Sacra, Valdeorras and Monterreim. In addition, try Txacoli, a wine from the northern Basque country, which is traditionally served with pintxos. It is a fresh, crisp, acidic and slightly fizzy wine. Look out also for wines from Rueda, in Castille and Leon – these are crisp, fine white wines that are as famous in Spain as reds from Rioja.

Rosé

Spanish rosé wines can be found from Rioja in the north to the more robust south. They tend to be dry, bright, fruity and refreshing, and sometimes quite full-bodied, so go well with chorizo, ham, seafood or mild cheeses.

Cava

This sparkling wine is a popular choice to serve with tapas. Most of it is produced in Catalonia, largely in Penedès. It can be white or rosé and produced in varying level of dryness, and is perfect to drink with olives, prawns, mushrooms, salamis and cheeses.

Sherry

Sherry is made in Andalucia, in the south, and is one of Spain's most popular aperitifs. There are three main types of sherry: dry, medium and sweet. As with wine the sherry regions are also governed by the *Denominaciones de Origen*. The dry sherries, Fino and Manzanilla, are pale in colour, extremely dry and have a delicate flavor. They are usually served with tapas as a starter and are perfect with tortilla, meatballs and chorizo tapas dishes. Then there is Amontillado, which is medium dry, has a golden amber colour and goes well with poultry, robust cheese and oily fish, while Oloroso is a darker, richer sherry, and is a perfect accompaniment to red meat.

Hygiene in the Kitchen

I t is well worth remembering that many foods can carry some form of bacteria. In most cases, the worst it will lead to is a bout of food poisoning or gastroenteritis, although for certain people this can be more serious. The risk can be reduced or eliminated by good food hygiene and proper cooking.

Do not buy food that is past its sell-by date and do not consume any food that is past its use-by date. When buying food, use your eyes and nose. If the food looks tired, limp or a bad colour or it has a rank, acrid or simply bad smell, do not buy or eat it under any circumstances.
Do take special care when preparing raw meat and fish.

A separate chopping board should be used for each food; wash the knife, board and the hands thoroughly before handling or preparing any other food.

Regularly clean, defrost and clear out the refrigerator or freezer – it is worth checking the packaging to see exactly how long each product is safe to freeze.

Avoid handling food if suffering from an upset stomach, as bacteria can be passed on through food preparation.

Dish cloths and tea towels must be washed and changed regularly. Ideally, use disposable cloths which should be replaced on a daily basis. More durable cloths should be left to soak in bleach, then washed in the washing machine on a boil wash.

Keep the hands, cooking utensils and food preparation surfaces clean and do not allow pets to climb onto any work surfaces.

Buying

Avoid bulk buying where possible, especially fresh produce such as meat, poultry, fish, fruit and vegetables, unless buying for the freezer. Fresh foods lose their nutritional value rapidly, so buying a little at a time minimises loss of nutrients. It also eliminates a packed refrigerator, which reduces the effectiveness of the refrigeration process.

When buying prepackaged goods such as cans or pots of cream and yogurts, check that the packaging is intact and not damaged or pierced at all. Cans should not be dented, pierced or rusty. Check the sell-by dates even for cans and packets of dry ingredients such as flour and rice. Store fresh foods in the refrigerator as soon as possible – not in the car or the office.

When buying frozen foods, ensure that they are not heavily iced on the outside and the contents feel completely frozen. Ensure that the frozen foods have been stored in the cabinet at the correct storage level and the temperature is below -18°C/-0.4°F. Pack in cool bags to transport home and place in the freezer as soon as possible after purchase.

Preparation

Make sure that all work surfaces and utensils are clean and dry. Hygiene should be given priority at all times. Separate chopping boards should be used for raw and cooked meats, fish and

vegetables. Currently, a variety of good-quality plastic boards come in various designs and colours. This makes differentiating easier and the plastic has the added hygienic advantage of being washable at high temperatures in the dishwasher. (NB: If using the board for fish, first wash in cold water, then in hot, to prevent odour!) Also, remember that knives and utensils should always be thoroughly cleaned after use.

When cooking, be particularly careful to keep cooked and raw food separate to avoid any contamination. It is worth washing all fruits and vegetables, regardless of whether they are going to be eaten raw or lightly cooked. This rule should apply even to prewashed herbs and salads.

Do not reheat food more than once. If using a microwave, always check that the food is piping hot all the way through. In theory, the food should reach a minimum temperature of 70°C/158°F and needs to be cooked at that temperature for at least 3 minutes to ensure that any bacteria in the food are killed.

All poultry must be thoroughly thawed before using, including chicken and poussin. Remove the food to be thawed from the freezer and place in a shallow dish to contain the juices.

Leave the food in the refrigerator until it is completely thawed. A 1.4 kg/3 lb whole chicken will take about 26–30 hours to thaw. To speed up the process, immerse the chicken in cold water. However, make sure that the water is changed regularly. When the joints can move freely and no ice crystals remain in the cavity, the bird is completely thawed.

Once thawed, remove the wrapper and pat the chicken dry. Place the chicken in a shallow dish, cover lightly and store as close to the base of the refrigerator as possible. The chicken should be cooked as soon as possible.

Some foods can be cooked from frozen, including many prepacked foods such as soups, sauces, casseroles and breads. Where applicable, follow the manufacturers' instructions.

Vegetables and fruits can also be cooked from frozen, but meats and fish should be thawed first. The only time food can be refrozen is when the food has been thoroughly thawed, then cooked. Once the food has cooled, then it can be frozen again. On such occasions, the food can only be stored for one month.

All poultry and game (except for duck) must be cooked thoroughly. When cooked, the juices will run clear from the thickest part of the bird – the best area to try is usually the thigh. Other meats, such as minced meat and pork, should be cooked right the way through. Fish should turn opaque, be firm in texture and break easily into large flakes.

When cooking leftovers, make sure they are reheated until piping hot and that any sauce or soup reaches boiling point first.

Storing, Refrigerating and Freezing

Meat, poultry, fish, seafood and dairy products should all be refrigerated. The temperature of the refrigerator should be between 1–5°C/34–41°F, while the freezer temperature should not rise above -18°C/-0.4°F.

Hygiene in the Kitchen

To ensure the optimum refrigerator and freezer temperature, avoid leaving the door open for a long time. Try not to overstock the refrigerator, as this reduces the airflow inside and affects the efficiency in cooling the food within. When refrigerating cooked food, allow it to cool down quickly and completely before refrigerating. Hot food will raise the temperature of the refrigerator and possibly affect or spoil other food stored in it.

Food within the refrigerator and freezer should always be covered. Raw and cooked food should be stored in separate parts of the refrigerator. Cooked food should be kept on the top shelves of the refrigerator, while raw meat, poultry and fish should be placed on bottom shelves to avoid drips and cross contamination.

It is recommended that eggs should be refrigerated in order to maintain their freshness and shelf life.

Take care that frozen foods are not stored in the freezer for too long. Blanched vegetables can be stored for one month; beef, lamb, poultry and pork for six months; and unblanched vegetables and fruits in syrup for a year. Oily fish and sausages can be stored for three months. Dairy products can last four to six months, while cakes and pastries can be kept in the freezer for three to six months.

High-risk Foods

Certain foods may carry risks to people who are considered vulnerable, such as the elderly, the ill, pregnant women, babies, young infants and those suffering from a recurring illness. It is advisable to avoid those foods listed below, which belong to a higher-risk category.

There is a slight chance that some eggs carry the bacteria salmonella. Cook the eggs until both the yolk and the white are firm to eliminate this risk.

Pay particular attention to dishes and products incorporating lightly cooked or raw eggs, which should be eliminated from the diet. Sauces including Hollandaise, mayonnaise, mousses, soufflés and meringues all use raw or lightly cooked eggs, as do custard-based dishes, ice creams and sorbets. These are all considered high-risk foods to the vulnerable groups mentioned above.

Certain meats and poultry also carry the potential risk of salmonella and so should be cooked thoroughly until the juices run clear and there is no pinkness left. Unpasteurised products such as milk, cheese (especially soft cheese), pâté and meat (both raw and cooked) all have the potential risk of listeria and should be avoided.

When buying seafood, buy from a reputable source which has a high turnover to ensure freshness. Fish should have bright, clear eyes, shiny skin and bright pink or red gills. The fish should feel stiff to the touch, with a slight smell of sea air and iodine. The flesh of fish steaks and fillets should be translucent, with no signs of discolouration.

Molluscs such as scallops, clams and mussels are sold fresh and are still alive. Avoid any that are open or do not close when tapped lightly. In the same way, univalves such as cockles or winkles should withdraw back into their shells when lightly prodded. When choosing cephalopods such as squid and octopus, they should have a firm flesh and pleasant sea smell.

As with all fish, whether it is shellfish or wet fish, care is required when freezing it. It is imperative to check whether the fish has been frozen before. If it has been frozen, then it should not be frozen again under any circumstances.

Fish  Shellfish Tapas

The range of fish and shellfish available, served either hot or cold, can add great variety to any tapas dish. The simple yet delicious flavours of Garlic Prawns are perfect on a warm summer evening. Or, if you fancy something a bit more warming, then Catalan Fish Stew or Fish & Chickpea Casserole will certainly hit the spot. From Seafood Salad to Galician-style Octopus ,even non-fish lovers are sure to find sumptuous morsels of seafood delight.

Chilli Prawns

Serves 4

450 g/1 lb raw giant prawns
with shells
1–2 red chillies, depending on
heat tolerance
freshly ground black pepper
4 tbsp Spanish olive oil
2 tbsp medium-sweet Spanish
sherry or 4 tbsp freshly
squeezed lemon juice
fresh flat-leaf parsley, roughly
chopped, for sprinkling
lemon wedges, to serve

Lightly rinse the prawns and place in a large, shallow dish, preferably in a single layer. Cut the chillies in half and carefully scoop out the seeds. (When handling chillies do not rub or touch your eyes before rinsing your hands thoroughly, as the oil from the chillies will make your eyes seriously sting and smart.) Roughly chop the chillies and scatter over the prawns together with the black pepper.

Blend the oil and the sherry or lemon juice together and pour over the prawns. Cover lightly and leave in the refrigerator for at least 30 minutes, or longer if time permits, spooning the marinade over a few times.

Preheat the grill or barbecue when ready to cook. Drain the prawns, place them in the grill pan or on the barbecue rack and cook for 8–10 minutes, turning them over occasionally until the prawns have turned pink. Spoon a little marinade over the prawns a couple of times during cooking.

Remove from the pan and arrange in a warm serving dish. Brush with a little of the marinade and scatter with the parsley and a few pieces of chilli from the marinade. Serve with lemon wedges to squeeze over.

Garlic Prawns

Serves 4

450 g/1 lb raw king prawns
sea salt
3 tbsp Spanish olive oil
4–6 dried red chillies, depending
on heat tolerance
6–8 garlic cloves
2 small bay leaves
3 small lemons, cut in half
150 ml/¼ pint dry white wine or
fish stock

Prepare the prawns by discarding the heads and shells but retaining the tail. Remove the black vein that runs down the back of each prawn. Rinse thoroughly and pat dry with absorbent kitchen paper.

Place the prawns on a large plate or dish and sprinkle with a little freshly milled sea salt. Leave lightly covered with kitchen paper in the refrigerator for at least 30 minutes.

When ready to cook, drain and rinse the prawns and pat dry with fresh kitchen paper.

Heat the oil in a large frying pan, then add the chillies and garlic and fry gently for 1 minute. Add the prawns to the pan and fry gently for 1 minute. Turn the prawns over and fry for a further minute.

Add the bay leaves to the pan together with the halved lemons and white wine or fish stock. Simmer for 5–6 minutes until the prawns have turned pink and the lemons are translucent. Spoon into a warm serving dish and serve.

Calamares

Serves 4

450 g/1 lb small squid
2–3 tbsp plain flour
sea salt and freshly ground
black pepper
4 medium egg whites
125 g/4 oz cornflour
about 600 ml/1 pint oil,
for deep frying
salad leaves and lemon wedges
(optional), to serve

Cook's Tip

If liked, after cleaning the squid,
rather than cutting into rings,
cut the squid into 5 cm/2 inch
pieces and score a diamond
pattern over the inside of each
piece. Fry these in the
same manner.

Clean the squid if necessary and cut into rings. Rinse lightly and pat dry with absorbent kitchen paper. Place the flour in a polythene bag and add seasoning to taste. Add the squid rings to the bag and shake lightly until the squid is lightly coated in the flour. Reserve while making the batter.

Lightly whisk the egg whites until frothy, then gradually add 1–2 tablespoons of the cornflour, beating well after each addition. Continue adding the cornflour and beating well until a light coating batter is achieved.

Heat the oil for deep frying in a large saucepan or deep-fat fryer to 180°C/350°F. Place 2 or 3 squid rings in the batter and coat lightly. Remove with a slotted spoon, allowing any excess batter to drip back into the bowl.

Carefully lower the squid rings into the hot oil and cook for 30 seconds, or until golden brown and crisp. Remove and drain on absorbent kitchen paper. Repeat until all the batter has been used. Keep the cooked squid warm in a low oven until all the rings have been cooked. Serve on a bed of salad leaves with lemon to squeeze over if liked.

Grilled Cuttlefish

Serves 4

4 fresh whole cuttlefish, cleaned
4 large garlic cloves, peeled
sea salt and freshly ground
black pepper
2 tbsp freshly chopped parsley
3 tbsp Spanish olive oil, plus extra
for brushing

Rinse the cuttlefish thoroughly and pat dry on absorbent kitchen paper, then cover lightly and place in the refrigerator until required.

Finely chop the garlic and place in a bowl. Add seasoning to taste and stir well. Add 1 tablespoon of the parsley.

Preheat the grill to medium and cook the squid for 3 minutes, brushing occasionally with a little extra oil if beginning to look dry. Spoon the parsley and garlic around the squid and continue to cook for a further 1–2 minutes until the squid is cooked. Serve sprinkled with any remaining parsley.

Galician-style Octopus

Serves 6–8

675 g/1¹/₂ lb octopus,
preferably frozen
4 large potatoes, scrubbed
4 tbsp Spanish olive oil
Spanish paprika,
for sprinkling

Bring a large saucepan of water to the boil. Remove any packaging from the octopus bag if necessary and place the octopus into the boiling water. Reduce the heat so that the water is simmering but not boiling and cook the octopus for 1 hour, or until soft. (If the octopus is fresh, freeze it first before cooking, as it is best used frozen for this dish.)

Once the octopus is tender and soft enough to eat remove from the heat and drain, then place in the refrigerator for at least 1 hour. Cut into small chunks and return to the refrigerator.

Cut the potatoes into slices about 5 mm/¹/₄ inch thick and cook in a pan of lightly salted water for 10–12 minutes until tender. (If liked, the potatoes can be peeled rather than scrubbed, cooked whole and then sliced once tender.)

Arrange the potatoes in the base of a serving dish and place the octopus pieces on top. Drizzle with the olive oil and sprinkle with the paprika.

Asturian Clams with Beans

Serves 4

225 g/8 oz dried broad beans
3 tbsp Spanish olive oil
2 garlic cloves, peeled and sliced
1 small onion, peeled
and chopped
2 small fresh bay leaves
few fresh parsley sprigs, plus extra
to garnish
$\frac{1}{4}$ tsp saffron strands
25 g/1 oz dried white breadcrumbs
450 g/l lb fresh clams
240 ml/8 fl oz water
salt
1 tsp sherry vinegar or white
wine vinegar

Soak the beans in a bowl of cold water for at least 8 hours, then drain, rinse and place in a saucepan. Add fresh water to cover. Bring to the boil and cook for 10 minutes, then drain.

Meanwhile, pour the olive oil into another large saucepan and add the garlic and onion. Add the herbs to the pan with the drained beans. Cover with fresh cold water, bring to the boil, reduce to a simmer, cover with a lid and cook for 1$\frac{1}{2}$ hours, or until the beans are tender. Discard the onion and herbs. Soak the saffron in a little warm water, then add to the beans. Sprinkle over the breadcrumbs and cook for 30 minutes, or until the beans are really tender.

Meanwhile, soak the clams in cold water to which a little salt and vinegar has been added for 15 minutes, then scrub the clams discarding any that are open. Place the clams in a deep frying pan or saucepan and cover with the water. Bring to the boil, cover with a lid and simmer for 10 minutes, or until the clams have opened, stirring occasionally. Discard any clams that remain closed.

Drain the beans and strain their liquor, mix both together and place in a warm serving dish. Spoon the cooked clams on top and serve garnished with fresh parsley sprigs.

Fisherman's Clams

Serves 4

36 fresh clams
4 garlic cloves
3 tbsp Spanish olive oil
300 ml/$^1/_2$ pint white wine and
water mixed together, or
150 ml/$^1/_4$ pint clam juice,
if available, and 150 ml/$^1/_4$ pint
white wine
2 tbsp fresh white breadcrumbs
parsley sprigs and lemon wedges,
to serve

Soak the clams in cold water put in a cool place or in the refrigerator until ready to use. Scrub the clam shells, removing any barnacles and discarding any that are open, then return to a bowl of cold water while preparing the other ingredients.

Peel and finely chop the garlic. Heat the oil in a large, heavy-based pan with a lid. Add the garlic and fry, stirring for 2 minutes, or until beginning to soften, taking care not to brown the garlic.

Drain the clams and add to the pan, stirring until all the clams are coated in the hot oil. Pour in the white wine and water or clam juice and white wine. Bring to the boil, cover with the lid, reduce the heat to low and cook, either shaking the pan or stirring the clams, for 5–8 minutes until the clams open. Discard any clams that do not open.

Sprinkle the breadcrumbs over the clams and shake or stir for a further minute. Spoon into a warm serving dish and serve garnished with parsley sprigs and with small pieces of lemon or lemon wedges to squeeze over.

Salt Cod Fritters

Serves 4

350 g/12 oz salt cod
450 g/1 lb potatoes, preferably a
floury variety such as King
Edward, peeled and chopped
240 ml/8 fl oz milk
1 onion, peeled and chopped
5 tsp Spanish olive oil, plus
150 ml/1 1/4 pint for frying
1 1/2 tbsp freshly chopped parsley
2 tbsp lemon juice
freshly ground black pepper
2 medium eggs
2 tbsp plain white flour
100 g/3 1/2 oz dried
white breadcrumbs
allioli and lemon wedges, to serve

Place the cod in a bowl and cover with cold water. Leave for at least 24 hours, or until dehydrated, changing the water frequently. Drain and pat dry.

Cook the potatoes in boiling water for 15 minutes, or until tender. Drain and mash.

Pour the milk into a pan and add half the onion and the cod. Poach for 10 minutes, or until tender, then remove, cool and discard the skin and bones. Flake into pieces and place in a bowl. Beat in the oil, then stir in a little potato, the remaining onion and the parsley. Gradually beat in the remaining potato, lemon juice, pepper and 1 egg.

Chill in the refrigerator, then shape into about 16 cakes and chill for 1 hour.

Dip the fritters into the flour, then the other beaten egg and coat in the breadcrumbs. Fry in the oil for 4 minutes, or until crisp, turning halfway through cooking. Drain and serve with the allioli and lemon wedges.

Mussels in White Wine ❧ Garlic

Serves 4

1.5 kg/3 lb fresh mussels
2 tbsp Spanish olive oil
4 garlic cloves, peeled
and chopped
1 medium onion, peeled
and chopped
300 ml/¹/₂ pint Spanish white wine,
or 150 ml/¹/₄ pint Spanish dry
white wine and 150 ml/
¹/₄ pint water
sea salt and freshly ground
black pepper
2 tbsp freshly chopped parsley

Place the mussels in a large bowl and cover with cold water. Place a plate on top and leave in a cool place or the refrigerator until required.

When ready to cook, drain the mussels and scrub well, removing any barnacles on the shells and pulling away the beards. Return to the rinsed bowl and fill with cold water. Discard any mussels that are open and do not close when tapped lightly on the surface.

Heat the oil in a heavy-based saucepan with a lid for 30 seconds. Add the garlic and onion and fry for 5 minutes over a low heat or until the onion has softened. Stir frequently, taking care that the onion does not burn. Pour in the wine and allow to come to the boil, then reduce heat to a simmer and cook for 3 minutes. Add seasoning to taste.

Drain the mussels and add the to the saucepan. Cover with the lid and cook for 5–8 minutes, stirring frequently, or until the mussels have opened. Discard any mussels that have not opened. Spoon into a warm serving dish and sprinkle with the parsley. Serve immediately.

Mussels in Escabeche

Serves 4

900 g/2 lb fresh mussels
150 ml/¹/₄ pint Spanish olive oil
4 garlic cloves, peeled
and chopped
1 medium onion, peeled and
thinly sliced
2 fresh bay leaves
150 ml/¹/₄ pint Spanish white wine
1 tsp paprika
3 tbsp sherry or white
wine vinegar
sea salt and freshly ground
black pepper
extra fresh bay leaves, to garnish
bread, to serve

Place the mussels in a large bowl and cover with cold water. Place a plate on top and leave in a cool place or the refrigerator for 2 hours.

Clean and cook the mussels using the oil, garlic, onion, wine and water as previously described on page 72. After draining the cooked mussels remove the mussel meat from their shells and reserve.

Pour the oil into a deep frying pan and cook the garlic and onion for 2 minutes stirring frequently until the garlic and onion are lightly brown. Reduce the heat to a simmer then add the bay leaves and wine. Cook gently for a further 2 minutes then add the paprika pepper, seasoning to taste with the sherry or vinegar and salt and pepper and simmer for 5 minutes stirring occasionally. Leave to cool for at least 5 minutes.

Meanwhile, arrange the mussel meat in a serving dish and spoon over the cooled sauce. Cover lightly and leave for the flavours to blend, overnight if possible.

When ready to serve, garnish with fresh bay leaves and serve with bread.

Ensaladilla

Serves 4

3 large potatoes, peeled
1 large carrot, peeled
125 g/4 oz French beans, trimmed
75 g/3 oz peas
2 bottled artichoke hearts
50 g/2 oz cornichons
2–3 tbsp capers, rinsed
1 red pepper, deseeded
175 g/6 oz canned tuna, drained

For the Mayonnaise

2 medium egg yolks
1 tsp ready-made mustard,
such as Dijon
150 ml/¼ pint Spanish olive oil
2 tbsp lemon juice
sea salt and freshly ground
black pepper
2 garlic cloves, peeled
and crushed

Cut the potatoes, carrot and beans into small chunks, ensuring they are all similar in size, then cook together with the peas in boiling water until tender. Drain and place in a bowl.

Cut the artichokes and cornichons into small pieces and thoroughly rinse the capers; add to the bowl of vegetables. Cut the pepper into a similar size and add to the other vegetables and stir well. Flake the tuna into small pieces and add to the vegetables. Cover and reserve.

Place the egg yolks into a bowl together with the mustard and whisk well. While continuing to whisk, slowly pour in the oil whisking throughout, adding a little lemon juice as the mayonnaise becomes thick.

When all the oil has been added, add seasoning to taste and the crushed garlic. Continue to add the lemon juice until a smooth, spreadable consistency is achieved.

Add the mayonnaise to the vegetables, stir lightly together and spoon into a serving dish. Cover and leave in a cool place until required.

Crab Leg Fritters

Serves 4

For the batter

125 g/4 oz plain white flour
pinch salt
1 tsp paprika
1 tbsp Spanish olive oil
150 ml/¼ pint cold water
2 medium egg whites
oil, for deep frying

For the crabs

8 medium soft-shell crab legs
2 tbsp plain flour

To serve

lettuce
tartare sauce or
chilli sauce (optional)

Sieve the flour, salt and paprika into a mixing bowl and make a well in the centre. Pour the oil and half the water into the well and gradually beat in the flour, drawing the flour into the centre of the well. Gradually add the remaining water and beat well to form a smooth batter. Allow to stand for at least 30 minutes.

Just before using, whisk the egg whites until stiff, then gradually stir into the batter.

Heat the oil in a deep-fat fryer to 180°C/350°F and have kitchen paper ready for draining.

Prepare the crab legs by rinsing well and drying, then coat in the plain flour. Dip in the batter and, using a slotted spoon, place in the oil. Cook for 4–5 minutes until golden brown and crisp. Remove and drain on kitchen paper. Repeat with the other crab legs. Serve warm on a bed of lettuce with tartare sauce or chilli sauce if liked.

Fish Chickpea Casserole (Potaje)

Serves 4

6 tbsp Spanish olive oil
1 Spanish onion, peeled
and chopped
2 leeks, trimmed, washed and
sliced into rings
1 fennel bulb, trimmed
and chopped
75 g/3 oz chorizo, diced
1 red chilli, trimmed and chopped
2 garlic cloves, peeled
and chopped
1 tsp sweet paprika
1 tbsp freshly chopped thyme
2 fresh bay leaves
few saffron strands
300 ml/^{1}/$_2$ pint fish stock
150 ml/^{1}/$_4$ pint Spanish white wine
200 g can chickpeas, drained
salt and freshly ground
black pepper
450 g/1 lb firm white fish, cut into
small pieces
2 tbsp chopped almonds

Heat the oil in a large pan and fry the vegetables and chorizo for 5 minutes. Add the spices, herbs and saffron and fry for a further 2 minutes.

Add the stock and wine, then the chickpeas, and add seasoning to taste.

Skin the fish if necessary and remove any bones. Add to the stew together with the chopped almonds. Place over a gentle heat and bring to the boil. Cover with the lid and reduce the heat to a simmer. Cook gently for 10–12 minutes until the fish and vegetables are tender, then serve.

Catalan Fish Stew (Suquet)

Serves 4

225 g/8 oz large raw prawns
225 g/8 oz fresh clams
450 g/1 lb fresh mussels
6 tbsp Spanish olive oil
1 Spanish onion, peeled
and chopped
1 fennel bulb, trimmed
and chopped
1 red chilli, trimmed and chopped
2 garlic cloves, peeled
and chopped
few saffron strands
2 fresh bay leaves
300 ml/^{1}/$_2$ pint fish stock
150 ml/^{1}/$_4$ pint Spanish white wine
salt and freshly ground
black pepper
450 g/1 lb firm white fish
flat-leaf parsley, to garnish

Clean the prawns and leave whole. Clean the clams and mussels, discarding any that are open. Keep in cold water until required.

Heat the oil in a large pan and fry the vegetables together with the chilli and garlic for 5 minutes. Add the saffron and bay leaves and fry for a further 2 minutes.

Add the stock and wine with seasoning to taste.

Skin the fish if necessary and remove any bones. Add to the stew together with the reserved prawns, mussels and clams. Bring to the boil. Cover with the lid and reduce the heat to a simmer.

Cook gently for 10–12 minutes until the fish and vegetables are tender. Discard any unopened mussels or clams. Serve garnished with flat-leaf parsley.

Marinated Fresh Anchovies

Serves 4–6

675 g/1¹/₂ lb fresh anchovies
300 ml/¹/₂ pint white wine vinegar
300 ml/¹/₂ pint Spanish extra
virgin olive oil
1 tbsp dried oregano
2 dried red chillies or 1 tbsp
crushed chillies
3 tbsp freshly chopped
flat-leaf parsley
3 garlic cloves, peeled
and crushed
1 tbsp sea salt
1 tsp freshly ground black pepper
flat-leaf parsley sprigs, to garnish

Using kitchen scissors, trim and discard all the fins from the anchovies. With a sharp knife, slit each anchovy along its belly and remove its innards. Rinse well.

Cut off the head and carefully pull out the spine and any pin bones from the top with your forefinger and thumb. Cut each fish into small fillets. Gently rinse in cold water and drain on absorbent kitchen paper.

Arrange the anchovies in the base of a large dish and sprinkle with 2 tablespoons of the vinegar. Continue with the layers of anchovies and vinegar. Once all the anchovies and vinegar have been used, cover and leave to marinate in the refrigerator for at least 4 hours.

Drain the anchovies, then rinse and pat dry. Place a layer of the anchovies in serving dishes. Pour over a little of the oil, oregano, chillies, parsley, garlic and seasoning. Repeat the layering until all the ingredients have been used. Cover and leave to marinate in the refrigerator for 2 hours.

Allow the anchovies to come to room temperature before serving and garnishing with parsley.

Fried Anchovies

Serves 4

1 kg/2¹/₄ lb fresh anchovies,
gutted, cleaned and split in half
3 tbsp plain flour
sea salt
300 ml/¹/₂ pint Spanish olive oil,
for frying
lemon wedges, to serve

For the allioli

1 medium egg yolk
pinch mustard powder
sea salt and freshly ground
black pepper
1 garlic clove, peeled
and crushed
150 ml/¹/₄ pint Spanish extra
virgin olive oil
1 tbsp lemon juice or white
wine vinegar

First, make the allioli. Place the egg yolk in a bowl and stir in the mustard powder and seasoning to taste. Beat well, then add the crushed garlic.

Using a whisk, gradually whisk in the oil, beating well after each addition. If the allioli is becoming too thick, stir in a little of the lemon juice. When all the oil has been added, stir in sufficient lemon juice to give a smooth coating consistency. Cover and store in the refrigerator until ready to use.

Rinse the fish and pat dry. Place the flour on a plate or in a polythene bag and add salt to taste. Coat the fish in the flour, then shake off any excess.

Heat the oil in a deep-fat fryer to 180°C/350°F. Place a layer of fish in the base of the frying basket. Lower the fish basket and fry for 3–5 minutes. Remove and drain on absorbent kitchen paper. Repeat until all the fish is fried. Serve with the prepared allioli and lemon wedges.

Ensaladilla Stuffed Eggs

Serves 4

8 medium eggs
3 tbsp Ensaladilla (*see* page 76)
sea salt and freshly ground
black pepper
shredded lettuce, to serve
16 olives stuffed with pimento, cut
in half (optional)
1 red pepper, skinned, or
16 canned anchovy fillets
(optional)

Place the eggs into a saucepan and cover with cold water. Bring to the boil and boil gently for 10 minutes. Remove from the hob and plunge into cold water.

Shell the eggs, cut in half, remove the cooked yolk and place in a bowl. Mash with a fork until smooth. Slowly add the Ensaladilla and stir into the mashed egg yolk. Add seasoning to taste and reserve.

Carefully fill the hollows in the halved egg white with the Ensaladilla mixture, forking the top to form a neat finish. Arrange some shredded lettuce in the base of the serving dish.

Place the stuffed eggs on top of the lettuce and arrange a halved olive and pepper strip or a canned anchovy on top. Serve.

Salt Cod Stuffed Peppers

Serves 4

450 g/1 lb salt cod
4 long sweet red peppers,
deseeded and blanched (or use
dried and rehydrate), plus 2 red
peppers, skinned
1 yellow pepper, skinned
2 garlic cloves
1 small Spanish onion
150 ml/¹/₄ pint Spanish olive oil
3 ripe tomatoes, chopped
¹/₂ tsp saffron strands
freshly ground black pepper
flat-leaf parsley, to garnish

Preheat the oven to 180°C/ 350°F/Gas Mark 4, 10 minutes before cooking. Prepare the cod as described on page 70. After soaking, cut the fish into 8 pieces, place in a dish, cover with cold water and leave until required.

Scoop out the flesh of he peppers and blend in a food processor. Reserve. Peel and slice the garlic. Peel and slice the onion.

Pour 150 ml/4 fl oz of the oil in a frying pan and heat. Add the garlic and simmer for 3 minutes, then remove the garlic and reserve. Drain the cod and pat dry, then cook in the garlic-flavoured oil on both sides for 3 minutes, remove and reserve.

Pour the remaining oil into a separate pan and add the reserved garlic, the onion and pepper flesh with the tomatoes and saffron and cook for 10 minutes, or until the onion and tomatoes are tender. Pass through a food processor and add black pepper to taste. Pour into an ovenproof dish.

Stuff the peppers with the cod and place on top of the sauce. Cover and heat in the oven for 25 minutes, or until hot. Garnish with the parsley and serve.

Catalan Cod Salad (Esqueixada)

Serves 4

450 g/1 lb salt cod
1 Spanish onion
1 red pepper
3 ripe tomatoes
salad leaves (optional)
12–16 pitted black olives
1 tsp sweet paprika
2–3 tbsp Spanish extra virgin
olive oil

Prepare and cook the salt cod as described on page 70. When cool, cut the cod into bite-size pieces, place on a plate, cover and leave in the refrigerator while preparing the other ingredients.

Cut the onion in half and thinly slice. Separate the onion slices and reserve.

Preheat the grill and line the grill rack with kitchen foil. Cut the pepper into quarters and discard the seeds. Place skin-side up on the foil-lined grill rack and cook for 8–10 minutes until the skins have blackened. Turn the peppers round to ensure all the skin is blackened. Remove and place in a polythene bag and leave for 10 minutes, then skin. Cut the pepper into small chunks and reserve.

Wash and cut the tomatoes into small chunks, discarding the seeds if preferred. Arrange the salad leaves (if required) in the base of a serving dish. Arrange all the prepared salad ingredients, including the cod and black olives. Sprinkle with the sweet paprika and drizzle over the oil. Cover lightly and keep in the refrigerator. Remove from the refrigerator 15 minutes before serving, to allow to come to room temperature, then serve.

Tuna Empanada

Serves 6–8

450 g/1 lb ready-made
shortcrust pastry
2 tbsp Spanish olive oil
675 g/1½ lb, onions, peeled
and sliced
2 garlic cloves, peeled
and crushed
2 tbsp sun-dried tomato paste
400 g can tuna in oil, drained
and flaked
3 tbsp single cream
50 g/2 oz Manchego cheese, grated
freshly ground black pepper
1 egg, beaten

Food Fact

Empanada is basically the Spanish
for 'pie'. They can be filled with all
kinds of fish, meat and vegetable
fillings. They come in slices or in
individual pies, a bit like pasties.

Preheat the oven to 200°C /400°F/Gas Mark 6, 15 minutes before baking. Roll out half the pastry on a lightly floured surface to form an oblong, 25 x 20.5 cm/10 x 8 inches. Place on a baking sheet. Chill for 10 minutes, then prick the base and bake in the oven for 15 minutes. Cool.

Heat the oil in a heavy-based frying pan, then add the onions and cook, stirring occasionally, for 15 minutes, or until browned. Add the garlic and cook for 5 more minutes.

Mix the tomato paste, tuna and cream together in a large bowl, then stir in the grated cheese and mix. Season with black pepper.

Pile the tuna mixture onto the cooled pastry base and spread evenly, then top with the cooked onions. Leave a border around the mixture. Brush the edge with beaten egg.

Roll the remaining pastry into a rectangle large enough to cover the tuna mixture and base. Place the pastry over the tuna filling. Trim the edges and press well to seal, then brush all over with the egg.

Bake for 35–40 minutes until crisp and golden brown. Serve cut into wedges.

Whitebait Pinchos

Serves 4

450 g/1 lb whole whitebait or
large anchovies
200 ml/7 fl oz sherry vinegar
1 garlic clove, peeled
and chopped
100 ml/3¹/₂ fl oz Spanish olive oil
juice of ¹/₂ lemon (about 2 tbsp)
1 tbsp freshly chopped parsley
sea salt and freshly ground
black pepper
4 rolls or thick slices of bread

Food Fact

Pinchos are small simple snacks that
are traditionally served in bars and
cafés throughout Spain, but
especially in northern Spain. They
can be made using fish, cheese,
eggs, meat or vegetables, and are
usually held together with a
cocktail stick.

Remove the head from the fish by pulling upwards (the innards will follow), then split the fish down the middle and remove the spine. Rinse lightly and pat dry with absorbent kitchen paper.

Place the whitebait or anchovies skin-side up in a dish and pour over the sherry vinegar so the fish are just covered. Leave for 15 minutes until the fillets turn white.

Remove from the vinegar and place into another dish. Mix the garlic, oil, lemon juice, parsley and seasoning together and pour over the fish. Lightly cover, then leave in the refrigerator for 1 hour.

If using rolls, cut in half, or halve or quarter the slices of bread. Serve one fillet on a half a roll or piece of bread. Add a cocktail stick and serve.

Tuna Red Pepper Montaditos

Serves 4

225 g/8 oz fresh tuna steak
3 tbsp Spanish olive oil, plus extra
for drizzling
2 tsp sherry vinegar
freshly ground black pepper
1 large red pepper
4 rolls or thick slices of bread

Food Fact

A montadito is a topping placed on a piece of bread. They are like pinchos, except they usually don't come with a cocktail stick to hold them together. They are very popular and can be found in most tapas bars throughout Spain.

Rinse the tuna steak and place in a shallow dish. Blend 2 tablespoons of the olive oil with the sherry vinegar and black pepper, then pour over the tuna. Cover lightly and leave to marinate in the refrigerator for at least 20 minutes.

Preheat the grill and line the grill rack with kitchen foil. Cut the pepper in half and remove and discard the seeds. Place the pepper skin-side up on the foil-lined rack and cook under the grill for 10 minutes, turning occasionally, until the skin is charred all over. Remove and place in a polythene bag and leave until cool. When cool, remove from the bag and skin. Cut into thin strips and reserve.

Heat a small frying pan, then add the remaining oil. Swirl the pan until coated in the oil. Drain the tuna and place in the frying pan. Cook for 3–4 minutes until just cooked. Remove from the pan and flake into small pieces.

Cut the rolls in half or the bread in halves or quarters, then drizzle with extra oil. Arrange the tuna and red pepper on top.

Cod, Red Pepper & Onion Montaditos

Serves 4

225 g/8 oz salt cod
1 Spanish onion
3 tbsp Spanish olive oil
4 soft rolls or 4 slices of
country bread
8 pitted black olives, sliced
1 Piquillo pepper
2 tbsp prepared mayonnaise
1 tbsp freshly chopped parsley
or chives

Cover the salt cod completely in cold water and leave to soak for 24 hours in the refrigerator. Discard the water and re-cover with water and soak for a further 2 hours.

Bring a pan of water to the boil, then drain the cod, rinse and add to the pan. Reduce the heat to a simmer and cook for 8–10 minutes until tender, then drain and leave to cool. Once cool, discard the skin and any bones, then flake into small pieces. Reserve.

Peel and thinly slice the onion. Heat half the oil in a pan and gently fry the onion, stirring frequently for 10–12 minutes until soft and translucent. Remove from the heat and drain on absorbent kitchen paper.

Cut the rolls in half, or the bread in halves or quarters and drizzle with the remaining oil. Arrange the cooked onion over the bread with the olives and top with Piquillo peppers, the cooked fish and a little mayonnaise. Sprinkle with parsley or chives and serve.

Red Pepper Cod Salad (Esgarraet)

Serves 4

225 g/8 oz salt cod
1 red pepper
1 Spanish onion
4 tbsp Spanish olive oil
1 tsp tomato purée
1 tbsp lemon juice
sea salt and freshly ground
black pepper
flat-leaf parsley sprigs, to garnish
toast, to serve

Soak the cod in plenty of cold water to cover for 24 hours, or longer if time permits. Leave covered in the refrigerator. When ready to use, drain and rinse. Place in a pan and cover with water. Poach for 8 minutes, or until tender. Drain and cool. When cool, remove and discard the skin and bones and divide into small chunks. Place in a bowl.

Preheat the grill and line the grill rack with kitchen foil. Cut the pepper into quarters and discard the seeds. Place the peppers skin-side up and grill for 10 minutes, or until charred. Turn the peppers round as necessary. Remove from the rack and place in a polythene bag for 10 minutes. Skin and cut into small chunks. Add to the cod.

Peel and chop the onion. Heat half the oil and gently cook the onion for 8–10 minutes until soft. Stir in the remaining oil with the tomato purée, lemon juice and seasoning to taste. Stir into the peppers and cod. Arrange spoonfuls of cod on a plate, garnish with parsley and serve with toast.

Shrimp Cakes (Tortas de Camaron)

Serves 4

175 g/6 oz dried shrimps
225 g/8 oz dried breadcrumbs, or
use tortilla crumbs
1/2 tsp salt
2–3 medium eggs
300 ml/1/2 pint oil, for frying

Cook's Tip

Dried shrimps can be found in
Asian and Mexican stores.
Keep the container tightly
closed, as they have a very
strong fishy aroma. The cakes
are cooked for special
occasions, especially around
Lent and Easter.

Place the dried shrimps with the breadcrumbs and salt in a food processor and blend until the shrimps are completely ground and well mixed together. Place in a bowl.

Beat the eggs, then gradually beat in sufficient egg, a little at a time, to form a thick consistency. Beat well after all the eggs have been added and a thick batter is formed (to a consistency of a thick porridge).

Pour in sufficient oil to come to about 1 cm/1/2 inch in a pan and heat. Place a generous tablespoon of the batter in the hot oil and fry for 3–4 minutes until golden. Remove with a slotted spoon and drain on absorbent kitchen paper. Repeat with the remaining batter. Serve warm.

Seafood Salad (Salpicon)

Serves 4

450 g/1 lb fresh mussels
225 g/8 oz salt cod
225 g/8 oz large cooked prawns
350 g/12 oz crabsticks
1 tbsp Spanish olive oil
125 g/4 oz courgettes, trimmed
and sliced
1 red pepper
125 g/4 oz black olives, pitted
sea salt and freshly ground
back pepper
2 tbsp Spanish extra virgin olive oil
1 tbsp white vinegar
fresh flat-leaf parsley, to garnish

Prepare and cook the mussels as described on page 72, remembering to discard any that are open before cooking and any that are closed after cooking. Prepare, soak and cook the cod as previously described on page 70.

Place the cooked mussels in a cool place and cover lightly. Discard any skin and bones from the cod, cut into small pieces and reserve.

Peel the prawns and cut the crabsticks into small lengths.

Heat the oil in a frying pan and cook the courgette slices gently for 3–4 minutes until softened, then drain and reserve. Discard the seeds from the pepper and cut into small chunks.

Arrange the seafood in a serving dish with the other ingredients. Add seasoning to taste. Blend the extra virgin olive oil and vinegar together, then drizzle over the salad. Garnish with parsley and serve.

Crab Montaditos

Serves 4–6

450 g/1 lb crab meat, thawed
if frozen.
2 tbsp freshly snipped chives
1 red pepper, deseeded and
finely chopped
1 small Spanish onion, peeled and
finely chopped
sea salt and freshly ground
black pepper
1 tsp tomato purée
175 ml/6 fl oz mayonnaise
1–2 tbsp Dijon mustard
grated zest and juice of
1 small lemon
1 baguette
1 tbsp Spanish extra virgin olive oil
1 tsp Spanish paprika

Gently squeeze the crab meat to remove any liquid, then place in a bowl. Stir in the chives, red pepper and onion with 1 teaspoon salt and mix lightly together.

Blend the tomato purée with the mayonnaise and gradually stir into the crab. Add the Dijon mustard with the lemon zest and juice. Add salt and pepper to taste, then mix well, cover lightly and reserve.

Slice the baguette into 8–12 thin slices and toast lightly. Drizzle with the extra virgin olive oil and top with the prepared crab mixture. Add a small sprinkle of paprika. Repeat with all the toast and crab mixture, then serve.

Crepe with Tuna, Pepper & Oregano

Serves 4

125 g/4 oz plain white flour
pinch salt
1 large egg
300 ml/1¹/₂ fl oz milk
2–3 tbsp oil, for frying

For the topping

2 red peppers
300 g/11 oz canned tuna
few salad leaves (optional)
50 g/2 oz pitted black olives
2 tbsp freshly chopped oregano

Sift the flour and salt into a mixing bowl and make a well in the centre. Add the egg and a little milk. Gradually beat to a smooth batter by slowly adding the remaining milk and drawing the flour in from the sides of the bowl. Reserve.

Prepare the topping. Cut the peppers in half and discard the seeds. Preheat the grill and line the grill rack with kitchen foil. Place the peppers on the foil-lined rack and cook under the grill for 10 minutes, or until the skins are blistered and black. Remove and place in a polythene bag and leave until cool, then skin. Cut into strips and reserve. Drain the tuna, flake into small chunks and reserve.

Heat a little oil in a small frying pan and, when hot, swirl the pan so it is lightly coated. Pour 1¹/₂ tablespoons of the batter into the pan and swirl again until completely covered. Cook for 2–3 minutes until the base is cooked. Turn or flip the crepe and cook the other side for 1–2 minutes until cooked. Remove and place on a plate. Keep warm while frying the remaining pancakes. Repeat with the remaining batter.

When the pancakes are cooked, arrange some salad leaves if liked on the crepe and top with the red pepper, tuna and olives. Sprinkle with the oregano, fold in half and serve.

Fried Fish Shrimp

Serves 4

900 g/2 lb assorted fish and
seafood such as mussels,
clams, large prawns, squid,
scallops, cod, monkfish
and anchovies
white wine and water to cook
mussels and clams
(*see* page 72)
50 g/2 oz plain white flour
1 quantity batter (*see* page 60)
Oil for deep-frying
lemon wedges and fresh herbs
to garnish
allioli (*see* page 182), and bread,
to serve

Prepare all the fish and seafood. Scrub the mussels and clams thoroughly, discarding any barnacles and beards. Leave in cold water until ready to cook. Discard any open ones. Peel the prawns if liked, cut the squid into rings and cut the scallops in half if large. Remove any bones from the fish and cut into small chunks. Rinse all the fish, including the anchovies, and pat dry on absorbent kitchen paper. Toss all the seafood and fish in the flour, except mussels and clams. Reserve.

Cook the mussels and clams as previously described on page 72. Remove the mussels and clams from the pan and, when they are cool enough to handle, remove the cooked seafood from their shells. Discard any that failed to open.

Heat the oil in a deep-fat fryer to 190°C/375°F. Working in batches, first coat the seafood and fish in the flour and then in the batter. Allow any excess to drip back into the bowl. Fry for 3–5 minutes until the batter is golden (the fish may take a little longer), turning over at least once. Drain on absorbent kitchen paper, garnish with lemon wedges and herbs and serve with allioli and bread.

Meat ❧

Poultry

Tapas

Meat and poultry ingredients give any tapas dish big flavours as well as adding an authentic, smoky dimension. The traditional Spanish ingredients of chorizo and Serrano ham allow for a wonderful salty taste that will enhance even the simplest of tapas selections. Why not try your hand at Catalan Sausage and Beans, or, if you want to experiment with something a little more adventurous, then opt for Chilli Snails, sure to be the talking point of any tapas selection!

Embutidos

Serves 4

A good selection of cold meats
including:
fuet
Serrano ham
Iberico ham
chorizo
pork loin (Lomo Embuchado)

Food Fact

Embutidos is the generic Spanish
term for charcuterie such as
salamis, chorizos and hams.

A platter of cured cold meats is often served as an integral part of a tapas meal. There are many types of cured meats in Spain, but here we have fuet, Serrano ham, Iberico ham, chorizo and pork loin. These can be increasingly found in some supermarkets, especially at the delicatessen counter, and in most specialist Spanish delicatessens.

If buying over the counter, make sure the meats are sliced properly and are neither too thick nor too thin. When laying them out on a plate, make sure they are properly separated. Sometimes a small amount of olive oil is drizzled over the meats – but not too much, as the meats contain quite a lot of their own oil already.

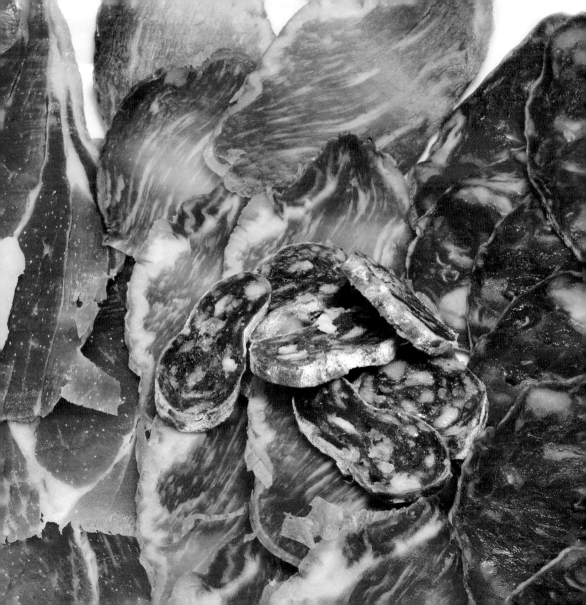

Mixed Tapas Platter

It is difficult to say how much to serve when dealing with a platter of food. Perhaps the best way, assuming you are catering for adults, is to allow 75–125 g/3–4 oz of meat and fish, and for the vegetables to allow a tablespoon each.

2 large Piquillo peppers
75 g/3 oz olives
50 g/2 oz anchovies
Serrano ham

Cook's Tip

Piquillo peppers are a variety of pimento and are sweet and not too spicy with plenty of flavour. Their name means 'little beak', as the pepper looks like a beak. They are grown in the north of Spain and, unusually today, are hand picked. They are roasted over an open fire to bring out their flavour and then packed in their own juices.

On a platter carefully separate the Serrano ham and arrange the slices in the centre. If liked, the ham can be rolled or lightly folded. As the ham is very thin, take care not to tear it or to leave it in a lump when it is difficult to separate.

Rinse 2 large, bottled red piquillo peppers, pat dry and place all together on the platter.

Rinse 75 g/3 oz olives in brine and arrange on the platter.

Open a 50 g/2 oz can of anchovies and drain well. Arrange on the platter, cover and leave in a cool place until required.

Chickpea Chorizo stew

Serves 4

2 tbsp Spanish olive oil
2 chorizo sausages, sliced
1 Spanish onion, peeled
and chopped
1 green pepper, deseeded
and chopped
3 garlic cloves, peeled and
finely chopped
1/2 tsp dried marjoram
400 g can chickpeas, rinsed and
drained
4 tsp sun-dried tomato paste
125 ml/4 fl oz Spanish dry
white wine
600 ml/1 pint chicken stock
sea salt and freshly ground
black pepper
25 g/1 oz fresh white breadcrumbs
freshly chopped flat-leaf parsley,
to garnish
crusty bread, to serve

Heat the oil in a casserole dish or large, deep frying pan over a medium-high heat. Add the chorizo and cook, turning, for 2–3 minutes until starting to crisp. Remove and drain on absorbent kitchen paper. Drain the excess oil and fat, leaving 2 tbsp in the pan.

Return the pan to a medium heat. Add the onion and green pepper and cook, stirring, for 5 minutes, or until softened. Return the chorizo to the pan with the garlic and marjoram. Stir for a further minute, then add the chickpeas and tomato paste blended with 2 tablespoons water. Pour in the wine and stock. Season with salt and pepper, then add the breadcrumbs, stir and bring to the boil. Reduce the heat to low and cook for a further 10 minutes, or until the sauce has thickened.

Garnish with chopped parsley and serve with crusty bread.

Pork Montaditos

Serves 4

225 g/8 oz pork loin
3 tbsp Spanish olive oil
1 garlic clove, peeled and crushed
¹/₂ tsp dried oregano
¹/₂ tsp ground cumin
¹/₂ tsp crushed chilli flakes
sea salt and freshly ground
black pepper
1 tbsp sherry vinegar
4 fresh bread rolls
1 tbsp Spanish extra virgin olive oil
fresh flat-leaf parsley sprigs,
to garnish
lemon wedges, to serve

Trim the pork loin if necessary, then cut into 4 portions.

Pour the oil into a small bowl, then add the crushed garlic, dried oregano, ground cumin and crushed chilli flakes. Season to taste with salt and pepper. Place the pork on a chopping board and rub this mixture into the pork pieces. Place the pork into a shallow dish.

Blend the sherry vinegar with the remaining oil and spices. Add a little more olive oil if there is only about 1 teaspoon. (You need about 3 tablespoons in total, including the sherry vinegar.) Cover lightly, then place in the refrigerator for at least 24 hours, or longer if time permits. Spoon or brush the marinade over the pork at least 5 or 6 times.

When ready to cook, preheat the grill and line the grill rack with kitchen foil. Drain the pork, place under the grill and cook on both sides for 2 minutes, then lower the heat and continue to cook for a further 6 minutes, or until completely cooked.

Meanwhile, split the rolls in half and drizzle the base with a little extra virgin olive oil. Top with a portion of pork and garnish with a sprig of parsley. Serve with lemon wedges.

Ham & Padrón Pepper Montaditos

Serves 4

225 g/8 oz Padrón peppers
2 tbsp Spanish olive oil
sea salt, for sprinkling
175 g/6 oz Serrano ham
4 slices crusty bread
fresh flat-leaf parsley sprigs, to
garnish (optional)

Cook's Tip

Padrón peppers literally melt in
your mouth when sprinkled with
a small amount of salt.

Lightly rinse the peppers and dry on absorbent kitchen paper.

Heat the oil in a frying pan and, when hot, add the rinsed and dried peppers. Cook, stirring frequently, for 8–10 minutes until the skins on all the peppers have blistered. Remove the peppers from the frying pan and place on a plate lined with absorbent kitchen paper. Reserve. When cool, skin and sprinkle with a little sea salt.

Fold the ham into small portions. Arrange the ham and both kinds of pepper on top of the toasted bread. Garnish with parsley, if liked.

Chorizo ❧ Padrón Pepper Pinchos

Serves 4

175 g/6 oz Padrón peppers
2 tbsp Spanish olive oil
sea salt
1 baguette, cut into slices
225 g/8 oz chorizo sausages

Lightly rinse the peppers and dry on absorbent kitchen paper.

Heat the oil in a frying pan and, when hot, add the rinsed and dried peppers. Cook, stirring frequently, for 8–10 minutes until the skins on all the peppers have blistered. Remove the peppers from the frying pan and place on a plate lined with absorbent kitchen paper. Sprinkle with a little sea salt. Reserve. In the meantime, cook the chorizo sausages in the frying pan.

Sprinkle the bread with a little Spanish extra virgin olive oil and arrange the Padrón peppers on top with the chorizo. Pin together with a cocktail stick and serve.

Figatell Pinchos

Serves 4–6

4 tbsp Spanish olive oil, separated
50 g/2 oz chorizo, chopped
1 medium red onion, peeled
and grated
1–2 garlic cloves, peeled
and crushed
3 fresh thyme sprigs, leaves
stripped and chopped
1 tsp freshly chopped flat-leaf
parsley
$^{1}/_{2}$–1 tsp smoked paprika
sea salt and freshly ground
black pepper
225 g/8 oz fresh beef or pork mince
1 baguette or soft rolls, to serve

Food Fact

Figatells is a Valencian word, and
they are basically little burgers.
This is a traditional recipe that is
popular along the entire
Mediterranean coast, with small
local variations.

Heat 2 teaspoons of the oil in a frying pan over a medium heat,
then add the chopped chorizo and stir frequently until the
chorizo is browned.

Add the grated onion and garlic to the pan together with the
chopped herbs and smoked paprika. Add salt and black
pepper to taste. Stir and add the beef or pork mince. Chill for
at least 30 minutes, lightly covered, in the refrigerator.

When ready to cook, shape the mixture into small, round
burgers, pressing firmly until the mixture sticks together.

Heat the remaining oil in a heavy-based frying pan and fry the
burgers over a gentle heat for 3 minutes, or until browned,
then turn the burgers over and fry for a further 3 minutes.
Continue to cook for 2–3 minutes until completely cooked.
Drain on absorbent kitchen paper. Place the burgers on a slice
of bread or a split soft roll. Insert a cocktail stick into the
burger to serve.

Chorizo Red Pepper Pinchos

Serves 4

1 large or 2 small red peppers
1 tsp fresh milled sea salt
50 g/2 oz chorizo, sliced
4–8 slices crusty bread
2 tbsp Spanish extra virgin olive oil
2–3 tbsp allioli (*see* page 182), or
crème fraîche
2–3 spring onions

Preheat the grill and line the rack with kitchen foil.

Cut the peppers into quarters and discard the seeds. Lightly rinse the peppers and dry on absorbent kitchen paper. Lightly score the skin with a sharp knife, taking care not to cut right through the flesh. Place skin-side up on the kitchen foil and cook under the preheated grill for 8–10 minutes until the skins are charred. Turn the peppers round a few times. Remove and place in a polythene bag and leave until cool enough to handle before stripping off the skin. Sprinkle the insides of the peppers with a little sea salt.

Roll the chorizo into a sausage shape. Place the bread on a serving platter and sprinkle with a little oil. Top with a piece of red pepper then a roll of chorizo. Spear with a cocktail stick to keep the ingredients in place.

Place the allioli or crème fraîche in a bowl. Trim the spring onions, then rinse and chop. Stir a little into the allioli or crème fraîche, then spoon a little on top of the pepper. Serve the remainder separately with the pinchos.

Cheese Ham Croquettes

Serves 4

2 tbsp unsalted butter

2 tbsp Spanish olive oil

1 medium onion, peeled and finely chopped

125 g/4 oz plain white flour, plus extra for dusting

175 ml/6 fl oz milk

75 g/3 oz Serrano ham, finely chopped

40 g/1½ oz Manchego cheese, grated

sea salt and freshly ground black pepper

3 large eggs

75 g/3 oz fresh white breadcrumbs

oil, for deep-frying

fresh flat-leaf parsley, to garnish

Gently heat the butter and oil in a medium saucepan over a medium heat until the butter has melted. Add the onion and cook for 5 minutes, or until the onion is soft, stirring occasionally. Slowly stir in the flour and cook for 2 minutes. Stir in the milk and cook, stirring constantly, for a further 3–4 minutes. Stir in the ham and three quarters of the cheese. Season with salt and pepper. Spoon the mixture onto a baking sheet, smooth the top and cool completely.

When ready to cook, whisk the eggs and pour into a shallow dish. Mix the breadcrumbs and remaining cheese together and place in another shallow dish. Scoop out tablespoons of the cooled mixture and, using floured hands, shape into 5 cm/ 2 inch ovals. Working with one oval at a time, coat in the beaten egg and then in the breadcrumb mixture. Transfer to a baking sheet lined with baking parchment. Repeat.

Heat 6.5 cm/2½ inches oil in a deep-fat fryer to 190°C/375°F and fry the croquettes, a few at a time, turning once, until dark golden brown, for about 1– 2 minutes. Using a slotted spoon, transfer to absorbent kitchen paper to drain. Serve warm, garnished with parsley sprigs.

Lamb Stew (Calderetta)

Serves 4

700 g/1¹/₂lb lamb thighs
4–6 garlic cloves, peeled
2 tomatoes
1 carrot, peeled and sliced
1 onion, peeled and chopped
1 fresh parsley sprig
1 bay leaf
1 tbsp Spanish olive oil
salt
fresh rosemary and parsley sprigs,
to garnish

For the sauce

1 tbsp Spanish olive oil
5 peppercorns
15 g/¹/₂ oz white breadcrumbs
2 whole cloves
1 tsp sweet Spanish paprika
¹/₄ tsp ground cumin

Cut the lamb into even-sized chunks and place in a large stew pot. Add about 750 ml/1¹/₂ pints water, or just enough to cover, then bring to the boil for 5 minutes, skimming off any scum or fat that rises to the top.

Add the garlic, tomatoes, carrot, onion, parsley and bay leaf to the pot, then add the olive oil and a pinch of salt. Simmer for about 50 minutes until the meat is tender. Drain off 300 ml/ ¹/₂ pint stock from the lamb.

Place all the sauce ingredients together in a food processor and process until blended.

Add the sauce ingredients to the lamb and cook for a further 5 minutes. Serve garnished with rosemary and parsley sprigs.

Lamb Chops (Costillas)

Serves 4

8 lamb chops
2–3 garlic cloves, peeled
and crushed
3 tbsp Spanish olive oil
1 tbsp white wine vinegar
sea salt and freshly ground
black pepper
few rosemary sprigs, plus extra
to garnish
fresh flat-leaf parsley, plus extra
to garnish
allioli (*see* page 182), to serve

If the lamb chops are very fatty, trim and remove some of the fat. (You need a little, as the fat helps to keep the meat tender.) Trim the chops, scraping off the meat from the bone, then rinse lightly, pat dry and place in a shallow dish.

Blend the garlic, oil and vinegar with seasoning to taste. Chop about 1 tablespoon of the rosemary and parsley and add to the marinade. Pour over the chops, cover lightly and leave to marinate for at least 30 minutes, or longer if time permits. Turn the chops over occasionally.

When ready to cook, preheat the barbecue, grill or griddle pan. Drain the chops, reserving the marinade, and cook for about 6–8 minutes on each side. The fat drippings may cause a flare, so take care. If a flare-up occurs, move the chop away from the flames, so it does not burn on the outside.

Garnish with extra rosemary and parsley sprigs and serve with allioli.

Tripe with Chickpeas

Serves 6

900 g/2 lb beef tripe
125 ml/4 fl oz white wine vinegar
225 g/8 oz pork belly, trimmed and cut into pieces
2 medium Spanish onions, peeled and roughly chopped
4–6 garlic cloves, peeled
2 bay leaves
6–8 black peppercorns
175 g/6 oz Serrano ham
225 g/8 oz chorizo
1–2 tbsp Spanish olive oil
1 tbsp Spanish paprika
225 g/8 oz morcilla, or use black pudding
2 tomatoes, chopped
400 g can chickpeas, drained
fresh flat-leaf parsley, to garnish
rustic bread, to serve (optional)

Clean the tripe under cold running water. Place in a bowl and cover with cold water and the vinegar. Leave for 10 minutes, then rinse thoroughly and cut into 7.5 cm/3 inch pieces.

In a heavy-based frying pan, add the tripe and pork belly. Cover with water and bring to the boil. Allow to boil for 1 minute, then discard the water. Re-cover the tripe with fresh water, about 600 ml/1 pint, and add 1 of the onions, half the garlic, the bay leaves and peppercorns. Bring to the boil, then reduce the heat and simmer for 3 hours.

Finely chop the remaining garlic and onion. Cut the Serrano ham into small cubes and slice the chorizo sausage into rounds. Fry the onion, garlic, ham and chorizo in olive oil for 5 minutes, or until the onion has softened. Remove from the heat and stir in the paprika. Add the mixture to the tripe. Cut the morcilla or black pudding into rounds and place in the pot together with the chopped tomatoes and chickpeas. Simmer for 15–20 minutes, garnish with parsley and serve with rustic bread, if liked.

Catalan Sausages Beans

Serves 4

450 g/1 lb dried white beans, such as haricot or cannelini, or use 400 g canned beans, drained and rinsed
2 botifarra (Catalan sausage)
3 tbsp Spanish olive oil, plus extra for serving
125 ml/4 fl oz allioli (*see* page 182)
1 tbsp freshly snipped chives

Soak the dried beans in a large bowl and cover completely with cold water. Leave to soak for at least 8 hours. Rinse and place in a large pan, cover with cold water and bring to the boil. Boil for 10 minutes, then discard the water, rinse and return to the pan. Re-cover with cold water, bring to the boil, then reduce the heat to a simmer and cook for 1½ hours, or until tender. Drain and reserve.

Preheat the grill and line the grill rack with kitchen foil. Place the sausages under the grill and cook for 6–8 minutes until cooked.

Fry the beans in the olive oil over a fairly high heat for 8–10 minutes until browned, turning them with a broad spatula to avoid bruising. It is essential to use olive oil, which imparts a special flavour and consistency to the beans.

When the beans are fried, pour a thin stream of olive oil over them, arrange on a warm serving platter and arrange the sausage on top. Garnish with a spoonful of allioli and a scattering of chives.

Meatballs (Albondigas)

Serves 4

450 g/1 lb fresh pork mince
1 small onion, peeled and chopped
1 garlic clove, peeled and crushed
1 tbsp freshly chopped oregano
or parsley
3–4 tbsp fresh white breadcrumbs
1 medium egg, beaten
sea salt and freshly ground
black pepper
1–2 tbsp plain flour, for coating
2–3 tbsp Spanish olive oil, for frying

For the sauce

1 small onion, peeled and chopped
2 garlic cloves, peeled and chopped
1 tbsp freshly chopped flat-leaf
parsley
1–2 tsp Spanish paprika
300 g/11 oz tomatoes, chopped
$1/2$ tsp saffron strands
125 g/4 oz frozen peas

Place all the ingredients for the meatballs, including salt and pepper to taste, into a bowl and, using your hands, bring the mixture together to form a ball. Alternatively, use a food processor and mix together using the pulse button. Remove and shape into small balls using a little flour.

Heat 1 tablespoon of the olive oil in a frying pan and add a few meatballs to the pan. Fry gently, turning, until golden brown on all sides. Remove from the pan and drain on absorbent kitchen paper. Repeat until all the meatballs are golden. Reserve.

For the sauce, fry the onion and garlic over a medium heat for 6–8 minutes or until the onion is soft. Add the parsley, paprika, tomatoes and saffron and pour in 300 ml/$1/2$ pint water. Bring to the boil, reduce the heat and simmer for 2–3 minutes to thicken. Season with salt to taste, then add the meatballs and peas to the pan. Simmer for 10 minutes to warm through, then serve.

Asturian Bean Stew (Fabada)

Serves 4

225 g/8 oz dried haricot beans
125 g/4 oz pork belly
6 garlic cloves, peeled and chopped
1 medium onion, peeled
and quartered
1 bay leaf
3 chorizo sausages
2 morcilla sausages
(black pudding will do)
6 small pork ribs (optional)
pinch saffron strands
1 tbsp Spanish paprika
salt (optional)
bread, to serve

Put the beans into a large bowl and cover with cold water. Leave to soak overnight.

The next day, drain the water from the beans and place in a large saucepan and cover with sufficient water so that it comes halfway up the sides of the saucepan. Add the all the other ingredients. Bring to the boil, reduce the heat and simmer for 2^1/$_2$–3 hours, or until the beans are tender. Taste, and if necessary add salt. Chorizo sausage and pork belly are salty, so you may not need to add any salt.

Cut the sausage into serving-size pieces and the pork ribs into single ribs. Serve with bread.

Spanish Garlic Chicken

Serves 4

1 whole roasting chicken, 1.5 kg/
3 lb, cut into even-sized pieces
3 tbsp Spanish extra virgin olive oil
3–4 garlic cloves
300 ml/¹/₂ pint Spanish dry
white wine
sea salt
300 ml/¹/₂ pint chicken stock
few fresh herbs sprigs, such as
chives, to garnish

Preheat the oven to 180°C/350°F/Gas Mark 4.

Rub the chicken pieces with 1 tablespoon of the extra virgin olive oil and place in a casserole dish.

Place the garlic cloves, 125 ml/4 fl oz of the white wine and salt to taste in a food processor and blend. Add 125 ml/4 fl oz of the stock and blend again until thoroughly mixed. Pour over the chicken. Cover the chicken with the lid and put in the oven on the centre shelf. Cook for 15 minutes, then baste the chicken joints with the cooking liquor. Re-cover with the lid and return to the oven and continue to cook for 15 minutes before basting again with the wine and stock. Continue to cook, uncovered, for 30 minutes, basting with the wine and stock. Take care that the liquor does not evaporate completely.

After 30 minutes, check that the chicken is thoroughly cooked. Serve garnished with the herbs and with the liquor as a sauce.

Chorizo in Wine

Serves 4

2 garlic cloves
1 red onion
350 g/12 oz chorizo
2 tbsp Spanish olive oil
2 tsp sun-dried tomato paste
50 ml/2 fl oz Spanish dry sherry or
Spanish dry white wine
1 bay leaf
1 tbsp roughly chopped
flat-leaf parsley
bread, to serve

Peel the garlic and red onion. Thinly slice the garlic and the red onion, then cut the onion slices in half to form half-moon shapes. Slice the chorizo thinly.

Heat the oil in a heavy-based frying pan and, when hot, add the sliced garlic and onion. Fry, stirring frequently, with a wooden spatula or spoon, and cook for 4–5 minutes until softened. Remove from the pan with a slotted spoon, leaving the oil still in the pan. Add the sliced chorizo to the pan and cook for 2–3 minutes until crisp.

Draw the pan off the heat. Blend the sun-dried tomato paste with the sherry or white wine, pour into the pan and add the bay leaf. Bring to the boil and allow to bubble for 3–4 minutes until the sherry or wine has reduced by half. Add the chorizo and heat for 1–2 minutes until hot, then add the chopped parsley to the pan.

Spoon onto a warm serving dish and serve with bread.

Meat Empanadas

Serves 4–6

450 g/1 lb puff pastry, thawed
if frozen
plain flour, for dusting
2 tbsp Spanish olive oil
450 g/1 lb onions, peeled and sliced
2 garlic cloves, peeled
and crushed
450 g/1 lb fresh pork mince
125 ml/4 fl oz tomato sauce
50 g/2 oz Manchego cheese, grated
freshly ground black pepper
1 small egg, beaten

Cook's Tip

If preferred, the empanadas can be
baked in a round dish and cut
into wedges.

Preheat the oven to 200°C/400°F/Gas Mark 6, 10 minutes
before cooking.

Roll out half the pastry on a lightly floured surface to an oblong of
25 x 20.5 cm/10 x 8 inches and place on a baking sheet. Chill for
10 minutes, then prick the base. Bake in the oven for 15 minutes. Cool.

Heat the oil in a heavy-based frying pan, add the onions and cook,
stirring occasionally, for 15 minutes, or until browned. Add the garlic
and mince and cook for 5–8 minutes until browned. Place in
a bowl.

Stir in the tomato sauce and grated cheese, then season with
pepper. Pile the mixture onto the cooled pastry base and spread
evenly, leaving a border around the mixture. Brush the edge with a
little of the beaten egg.

Roll the remaining pastry into a rectangle large enough to cover the
beef mixture and base. Place the pastry over the beef filling. Trim the
edges and press well to seal, then brush all over with the egg.

Bake for 35–40 minutes until crisp and golden brown. Serve cut
into squares.

Catalan Beans, Ham Chorizo

Serves 4

2 medium onions
450 g/1 lb lean bacon
75 ml/3 fl oz Spanish olive oil
125 g/4 oz chorizo
900 g/2 lb young broad beans
75 ml/3 fl oz Spanish white wine
1 bay leaf
sea salt and freshly ground
black pepper
1 tsp sugar, or to taste
150 ml/¹/₄ pint mix anisette
and muscatel
fresh mint sprigs, to garnish

Peel and finely chop the onions. Roughly chop half the bacon. Heat the oil in a heavy-based saucepan, add the onions and fry for 3 minutes, then add the chopped bacon and cook for 5–8 minutes until golden, stirring frequently.

Slice the chorizo and add to the saucepan together with the broad beans. Stir well until lightly coated in the oil, then pour in the white wine and add the bay leaf.

Separate the remaining bacon and add to the saucepan. Cover with a lid and simmer gently for 5 minutes. Add black pepper, sea salt and sugar to taste and continue to cook for 10 minutes, or until the beans are tender.

Pour in the anisette and muscatel mix, heat for 2–3 minutes, then serve garnished with a mint sprig.

Andalucian Beans Ham

Serves 4

1 kg/2.2 lb fresh or frozen
broad beans
125 g/4 oz Serrano ham
4 garlic cloves
1 medium onion
125 ml/4 fl oz Spanish olive oil
sea salt and freshly ground
black pepper
flat-leaf parsley, to garnish
warm chunky bread, to serve

Shell the beans if fresh and rinse. Bring a large pan of water to the boil and add the fresh or frozen beans. Cook the fresh beans for 10–12 minutes until tender, or the frozen broad beans for 12–15 minutes. Drain and allow to cool. When cool, split the outer casings, remove the beans and reserve.

Chop the Serrano ham into small strips or pieces (or leave whole if liked). Peel and finely chop the garlic and onion.

Heat a large frying pan, then pour in the oil. Heat until hot, then add the garlic cloves and onion. Cook, stirring, for 4–5 minutes until softened, then add the broad beans and Serrano ham and fry for 1 minute. Reduce the heat to a simmer and season to taste.

Cover with a lid and simmer gently for 15–20 minutes until the broad beans are really tender.

Add seasoning to taste, then stir and spoon into a warm serving dish. Garnish with the flat-leaf parsley and serve with warm chunky bread.

Broken Eggs (Huevos Rotos)

Serves 4

1 onion
4 large garlic cloves
4 tbsp Spanish extra virgin olive oil
450 g/1 lb potatoes
1 small pepper
4 tbsp freshly chopped parsley
4 large eggs
sea salt and freshly ground
black pepper
225 g/8 oz Serrano ham

Peel the onion and garlic, then finely chop the onion and crush the garlic. Pour the oil into a heavy-based frying pan and fry the onion and garlic over a medium heat for 5 minutes, stirring frequently. Remove and reserve.

Peel the potatoes if preferred, then slice thinly. Deseed the pepper and discard the seeds. Chop. Remove and reserve. Arrange the potatoes in the base of the pan and spoon over the onion, garlic and pepper, then sprinkle with the chopped parsley. Reduce the heat to a simmer, cover with a lid and cook gently for 20–25 minutes until the potatoes are tender and beginning to brown.

Crack the eggs over the potatoes and turn the heat down very low. Cover and cook the eggs for 5 minutes, or until the whites have just set. Break the yolks and remove from the heat. Season with salt and pepper and serve with thin slices of Serrano ham.

Flamenco Eggs

Serves 4

125 g/4 oz fresh shelled or
frozen peas
300 g/11 oz potatoes, peeled
and chopped
3 tbsp Spanish olive oil
1 small onion, peeled and chopped
2–3 plump garlic cloves, peeled
and chopped
125 g/4 oz chorizo and
Serrano ham, chopped
2 tomatoes, chopped
1 small red pepper, deseeded
and chopped
4–6 roasted Piquillo peppers
sea salt
6 large eggs

Preheat the oven to 200˚C/400˚F/Gas Mark 6, 15 minutes
before cooking. Cook the peas in boiling water for
5–6 minutes. Drain and reserve. Cook the potatoes in boiling
water for 8 minutes, or until just tender. Drain, return the pan to
the heat for 1–2 minutes to dry the potatoes, then reserve.

Heat half the oil in a frying pan and fry the potatoes for
3 minutes, then add the chopped onion, garlic and half of the
chorizo and Serrano ham. Continue to fry for 5 minutes.

Add the chopped tomatoes with the peas, red pepper and
Piquillo peppers and season with salt to taste. In a separate
pan, fry the rest of the chorizo and Serrano ham in the
remaining oil for 5 minutes. Reserve.

Spoon the potato mixture into six ovenproof dishes and crack
an egg on top of each. Place in the oven and cook for
12–15 minutes until the eggs are set to personal preference.
Serve immediately, garnished with the reserved chorizo
and ham.

Chicken Chorizo

Serves 4

4 chicken breast fillets
sea salt and freshly ground
black pepper
1 tbsp unsalted butter
3 tbsp Spanish olive oil
1 medium onion, peeled
and chopped
2 garlic cloves, peeled and crushed
1 tbsp tomato purée
450 ml/³/₄ pint chicken stock
2 medium tomatoes, skinned,
deseeded and chopped
225 g/8 oz chorizo, chopped into
bite-size pieces
4 roasted piquillo peppers, chopped
bread, to serve

Rinse the chicken and pat dry, then season with salt and pepper. Melt the butter with the oil, add the chicken and cook, turning occasionally, until the chicken is browned. Drain and place on a plate and lightly season again.

Add the onion and garlic to the oil remaining in the frying pan and cook, stirring frequently, for 5 minutes, or until the onion has softened. Return the chicken to the pan together with any chicken juices which are on the plate.

Blend the tomato purée with the chicken stock and gradually pour over the chicken. Stir in the chopped tomatoes, chorizo and chopped piquillo peppers. Bring to the boil, then reduce the heat to a simmer and cover with a lid. Cook for 20–25 minutes until the chicken is thoroughly cooked. Serve with fresh bread.

Chicken Chorizo Kebabs

Serves 4

2 large skinless, boneless
chicken breast fillets
3 tbsp Spanish olive oil
1 tsp sugar
1 tbsp tomato purée
2 tbsp sherry vinegar
$^1/_2$ tsp saffron strands
sea salt and freshly ground
black pepper
2–3 garlic cloves, peeled
and crushed
1 Spanish onion, peeled
and chopped
2 fresh bay leaves
1 small red pepper
125 g/4 oz chorizo
4 spring onions, trimmed
and chopped
lettuce, to serve

Rinse the chicken and pat dry with absorbent kitchen paper. Cut the chicken into small chunks and place in a shallow dish.

Blend the olive oil, sugar, tomato purée and vinegar together with the saffron, seasoning, garlic and chopped onion. Stir, then pour over the chicken and add the bay leaves. Cover lightly and leave to marinate for at least 30 minutes, spooning the marinade occasionally over the chicken.

Cut the pepper into quarters, deseed and cut into chunks or wide strips. Cut the chorizo into chunks.

When ready to cook, preheat the grill or barbecue and, if using the grill, line the grill rack with kitchen foil. Drain the chicken, reserving any marinade. Soak 4 long bamboo skewers. Thread the chicken pieces, red pepper and chorizo onto the presoaked skewers, not packing each skewer too tightly, so that the heat will penetrate.

Brush with the reserved marinade and cook either under the grill or on the barbecue, turning frequently and brushing with the marinade, for 10–12 minutes until the chicken is thoroughly cooked. Sprinkle with the chopped spring onions and serve on a bed of lettuce.

Chilli Snails

Serves 4

3 tbsp Spanish olive oil

3 fresh mint sprigs

1.5 kg/3 lb snails, look for the Bubé kind, cleaned inside and outside

2 garlic cloves, peeled and crushed

2 dried red chillies

1 red pepper

1 yellow pepper

sea salt and freshly ground black pepper

warm bread, to serve

Place a large saucepan over a low heat and add 1 tablespoon of the oil and the mint sprigs. Make sure the pan is large enough to hold all the snails.

Add the snails while the oil is still cool and cover with a lid. (This will stop the snails from escaping.) Leave for 1 minute. Remove the lid and stir again. Continue to heat, stirring frequently, and re-covering with the lid after each stir.

Once you can see the oil in the bottom of the saucepan, add the garlic and chillies and stir. Cook over a low heat for 45–60 minutes.

Cut the peppers in half and discard the seeds. Cut each pepper into small chunks. Add to the saucepan for the last 20 minutes of cooking time, stirring occasionally. Add seasoning to taste, then serve with chunks of warm bread.

Chorizo & Lentils

Serves 4

2 tbsp Spanish olive oil
1 tbsp Spanish paprika
2–3 plump garlic cloves, peeled
and chopped
225 g/8 oz chorizo, sliced into
small chunks
1 medium onion, peeled and
finely chopped
2 celery stalks, trimmed and sliced
1 red pepper, deseeded
and chopped
2 tbsp tomato purée
1 litre/1³/₄ pints chicken stock
4 tomatoes, chopped
300 g/11 oz lentils
salt and freshly ground
black pepper
1 tbsp freshly chopped
flat-leaf parsley
crusty bread, to serve

Heat the oil in a large, heavy-based saucepan over a gentle heat. Add the paprika together with the garlic and cook for 30 seconds before adding the chunks of chorizo, the onion, celery and chopped red pepper. Cook, stirring, for 2–3 minutes until the chorizo begins to sizzle and has browned.

Blend the tomato purée with the chicken stock, then pour into the saucepan. Add the chopped tomatoes and the lentils, and bring to the boil. Cover with a lid and reduce the heat to a simmer. Cook for 1 hour, adding more water if the stew is becoming too thick. Season to taste with salt and black pepper and stir in the chopped parsley. Serve the stew in warm bowls with crusty bread.

Chorizo, Morcilla, Pork ❧ Lentils

Serves 4

2 tbsp Spanish olive oil
1 tbsp Spanish paprika
2 garlic cloves, peeled
and chopped
1 Spanish onion, peeled
and chopped
125 g/4 oz chorizo, chopped
300 g/11 oz pork fillet, cut into
small chunks
225 g/8 oz black pudding, cut into
small pieces
2 celery stalks, trimmed and sliced
1 large carrot, peeled and chopped
2 tbsp tomato purée
1 litre/1³/₄ pints chicken stock
4 tomatoes, chopped
300 g/11 oz yellow lentils
sea salt and freshly ground
black pepper
crusty bread, to serve

Heat the oil in a large, heavy-based saucepan over a gentle heat. Add the paprika together with the garlic and onion, then cook for 30 seconds before adding the chunks of chorizo, pork and black pudding, the celery and chopped carrot. Cook, stirring, for 2–3 minutes until the chorizo begins to sizzle and has browned.

Blend the tomato purée with the chicken stock, then pour into the saucepan. Add the chopped tomatoes and the yellow lentils, and bring to the boil. Cover with a lid and reduce the heat to a simmer. Cook for 1 hour, adding more water if the stew is becoming too thick. Season to taste with salt and black pepper. Serve the stew in warm bowls with crusty bread.

Meatballs in Stock

Serves 8

1 kg/2¼ lb beef bones
2 carrots, peeled and chopped
2 onions, peeled and chopped
2 celery stalks, trimmed
and chopped
1 tbsp Spanish olive oil
few peppercorns
2 fresh bay leaves
1 bouquet garni
meatballs (*see* page 142)
sea salt and freshly ground
black pepper
1 tbsp freshly chopped
flat-leaf parsley
fresh bread, to serve

Preheat the oven to 200°C/400°F/Gas Mark 6, 15 minutes before using.

Place the bones in a roasting tin and roast for 1 hour, or until the bones are golden brown. At the same time, roast the carrots, onions and celery with a little oil for 30 minutes, or until golden.

Place both the bones and vegetables in a large saucepan together with the peppercorns, bay leaves and bouquet garni and cover with water.

Place over a medium heat and bring to the boil. Skim off the scum that rises to the surface, then cover with a lid and simmer for 3–4 hours, skimming off any scum that rises to the surface. Strain and reserve while preparing and cooking the meatballs.

Heat the prepared stock and, when hot, serve a bowl of stock with a meatball placed in the centre. Add seasoning to taste, then sprinkle with chopped parsley and serve with bread.

Spanish Sausages

A variety of small Spanish
sausages, including:
white pork sausages (bottifarra)
chorizo
morcilla

Whether large or small, hot and fiery or sweet and mild, Spanish sausages are a popular dish found in tapas bars. Distinct from cured meats, there are many different types of regional sausages available, from varieties of small sausages that are linked together, to large individual ones. Here we have three of the best-known: chorizo, which is made using the best pork meat, garlic and Spanish paprika; botifarra, a Catalan white sausage; and morcilla, a black pudding sausage.

In Spain, most tapas bars have a metal griddle (called a plancha) or frying pan at the back of the restaurant, where the sausages can be quickly cooked to order. If you are hoping to have Spanish sausages as part of your tapas menu, then look for them in a specialist Spanish shop, though some supermarkets now sell them. Simply fry them and serve.

Spanish sausages can also be served in a roll. A popular variation is bottifarra with morcilla in the same roll and is called 'blanco y negro' (black and white).

Chorizo Pepper Tortilla

Serves 8

450 g/1 lb potatoes, peeled
2 tbsp Spanish olive oil
1 Spanish onion, peeled
2–3 garlic cloves, peeled
175 g/6 oz chorizo, diced
2 red peppers, deseeded and
skinned (*see* page 130)
10 medium eggs
sea salt and freshly ground
black pepper
herbs, to garnish (optional)
warm chunky bread, to serve

Cook's Tip

The tortillas can be cooked in a small frying pan and served whole. This mixture will make about 6 small tortillas.

Cook the potatoes for 10–12 minutes until tender. Drain and reserve.

Heat the oil in a large, deep frying pan and, when hot, add the onion and garlic and gently fry for 8 minutes until softened. Remove and reserve.

Add the chorizo to the frying pan and cook, stirring, for 3 minutes, then add the reserved potatoes, onions, garlic and the red peppers. Stir all the ingredients together, then fry gently for a further 3 minutes.

In a bowl, beat the eggs with seasoning to taste and 3 tablespoons of water then slowly pour into the pan. Cook over a medium heat for 5 minutes or until the base has set, stirring the eggs with a fork while cooking.

Reduce the heat to low and cook for a further 10 minutes, or until the eggs are completely set. Test with a knife. If liked, brown the top under a preheated grill.

When set, cool for 10 minutes, then turn out and cut into small chunks. Garnish with herbs if liked, and serve with crusty bread.

Vegetable, Cheese & Egg Tapas

Whether a vegetarian or a vegetable lover, there are plenty of exciting and delicious vegetarian treats to be tried in this chapter. Patatas Bravas classically served with Allioli is a staple of even the most extravagant tapas selection. If you want to add another dimension to your dishes, then why not try Red Pepper Salad or Chickpeas with Spinach? Not only do they taste great but they will give your menu a splash of colour and vibrancy.

Garlic Mushrooms

Serves 6

450 g/1 lb closed cup mushrooms
1 medium onion
4 garlic cloves
1 hot green chilli pepper (optional)
2 tbsp Spanish olive oil
150 ml/¼ pint Spanish white wine
sea salt and freshly ground
black pepper
1 tbsp freshly chopped
flat-leaf parsley
warm chunky country bread,
to serve

Wipe the mushrooms with kitchen paper and trim the stalks. Reserve. Peel and chop the onion and garlic and slice the chilli, if using.

Heat the oil in a heavy-based frying pan and add the onion, garlic and chilli, if using, and gently fry for 5–6 minutes until beginning to soften, stirring occasionally. Add the mushrooms and cook, stirring frequently, until coated in the oil.

Pour in the white wine and bring to the boil. When the wine is bubbling, reduce the heat to a gentle simmer and cover with the lid. Cook for 10 minutes, or until the mushrooms are tender.

Add seasoning to taste, stir well, then spoon into a warm serving dish or casserole dish. Sprinkle with the chopped parsley and serve with chunks of warm country bread.

Pisto

Serves 4–6

1 medium aubergine
sea salt and freshly ground
black pepper
1 large onion
2–3 garlic cloves
2 red peppers
6 ripe medium tomatoes, skinned
2 medium courgettes,
about 225 g/8 oz
3–4 tbsp Spanish olive oil
freshly chopped herbs, to garnish
crusty bread slices, to serve

Trim the aubergine and slice thinly. Arrange in layers in a colander, sprinkling each layer with salt. Leave for at least 30 minutes, then rinse the salt off and pat dry with absorbent kitchen paper. Peel and slice the onion and garlic. Deseed the peppers and cut into small strips. Cut the tomatoes in half, scoop out the seeds, then chop. Trim the courgettes, peel if preferred, and slice thinly.

Heat the oil in a large, heavy-based saucepan for 2 minutes, then add the aubergine along with the onion and garlic. Cook over a gentle heat for 10 minutes, then add the tomatoes. Cover with a lid and cook, stirring occasionally, for a further 10 minutes.

Check that the vegetables are tender, then season to taste. Spoon into a serving dish, garnish with fresh herbs if liked, and serve with crusty bread.

Allioli

Makes 150 ml/¹/₄ pint

1 medium egg yolk, free range and
as fresh as possible
¹/₂ tsp mustard powder, or to taste
¹/₄ tsp salt, or to taste
¹/₄ tsp freshly ground black pepper,
or to taste
¹/₂ tsp caster sugar, or to taste
150 ml/¹/₄ pint olive oil
1 tsp lemon juice, or to taste
1–2 tsp warm water
2–3 garlic cloves, peeled
and crushed

Food Fact

This is the classic Spanish
condiment. It goes well with
roasted meats and is often
served on the side of certain rice
dishes. It is often served with just
bread as an additional tapa.

Put the egg yolk in a bowl, add the mustard powder with
the seasoning to taste, and half the sugar. Beat the egg
yolk until the mixture is creamy.

Slowly whisk in the oil, drop by drop, whisking throughout.
Continue until all the oil has been used. Add a little lemon
juice or water during this time if the mayonnaise is getting
very thick and it is difficult to add more oil.

When all the oil has been added, stir in sufficient warm
water to give a smooth consistency; it should drop easily
back into the bowl when a spoonful is dropped over the
bowl. Stir in the crushed garlic. Cover and store in the
refrigerator until required.

Pisto Montaditos

Serves 4–6

half quantity of freshly made pisto
(*see* page 180)
sea salt and freshly ground
black pepper
50 g/2 oz Manchego cheese
8–12 thick bread slices from a
long crusty loaf
2 tbsp Spanish olive oil
8–12 olives, preferably pitted

Place the prepared pisto into a saucepan and add sea salt and black pepper, to taste. Heat through gently, stirring occasionally. Take care that the pisto does not burn onto the base of the pan.

Cut the cheese into small pieces, and when the Pisto is heated through, add the cheese and stir. Remove from the heat.

Cut the bread into 5 cm/2 inch slices and drizzle the tops of the bread with the olive oil. Spoon the pisto on the top of each slice. Top each with an olive, insert a cocktail stick through the middle and serve.

Grilled Spring Onions (Calcots)

Serves 6

1.25 kg/2¹/₂ lb spring onions
2 dried red chillies
2 slices white bread
50 ml/2 fl oz sherry vinegar
6 ripe tomatoes
2 garlic cloves
1 fresh mint sprig
25 g/1 oz toasted
chopped hazelnuts
125 ml/4 fl oz Spanish olive oil
sea salt and freshly ground
black pepper

Food Fact

Romesco sauce is another of
the great Spanish condiments.
It originates from Tarragona
in Catalonia.

Preheat the barbecue. Trim the spring onions, discarding the roots. Wash well and pat dry with absorbent kitchen paper. Place in lines on the rack over the hot charcoal and cook for about 5 minutes, turning gradually so that they turn crisp on the outside and are cooked through inside. (In the kitchen, they can be cooked in a cast-iron frying pan or griddle pan.) Serve on hot tiles to keep in the heat, with a bowl of the sauce.

Meanwhile, make the romesco sauce to go with the calcots. Soak the dried red chillies for 30 minutes in sufficient water to cover, then drain. Soak the bread in the vinegar.

Preheat the grill and line the grill rack with kitchen foil.

Cut the tomatoes in half and peel the garlic cloves, then place the tomatoes on the barbecue or the grill rack and cook until softened. Crush the garlic with the mint, hazelnuts, soaked red chillies and soaked bread in a pestle and mortar. Once a paste has formed, add the tomatoes and continue to work until a smooth sauce is made. Gradually add the oil to form a paste, then add salt and pepper, to taste. Serve with the cooked spring onions.

Catalan Bread Tomatoes

Serves 4

1 freshly baked baguette
3–4 garlic cloves
1–2 tbsp Spanish extra virgin
olive oil
450 g/1 lb ripe tomatoes
sea salt and freshly ground
black pepper
$^{1}/_{2}$ tsp caster sugar

Cook's Tip

Small pieces of chopped cheese,
chorizo or ham can be added, if
liked. If preferred, a round
crusty loaf can be used in place
of the baguette.

Slice the bread into 10 cm/4 inch pieces and then cut horizontally in half. Toast the bread under a hot grill or on a hot barbecue. Peel the garlic and cut each clove in half. Rub the cut surface of the bread with the garlic cloves. Make sure that the bread is well coated in the garlic. Drizzle over a little extra virgin olive oil just before topping with the tomato.

Rinse and dry the tomatoes, then skin if preferred. To do this, make a cross at the top of each tomato and place in a heatproof bowl. Pour in sufficient boiling water to completely cover. Leave for 30–60 seconds until the skins start to crinkle and come away from the tomatoes. Drain, and allow to cool for a few minutes before peeling. Either slice or chop finely. Add salt and pepper, to taste and a little sugar to help bring out the flavour of the tomato.

Spoon the tomato on top of the bread slices and serve with extra oil to drizzle over.

Vegetable Coca

Makes 10

1 Spanish onion
2 garlic cloves
2 tbsp Spanish olive oil
fresh rosemary sprigs
1 small red pepper
1 small yellow pepper
1 small green pepper
1 courgette
4 medium ripe tomatoes
salt and freshly ground
black pepper
10 x 10 cm/4 inch prepared
pizza bases
fresh herbs, to garnish (optional)

Food Fact

Cocas are a Valencian or Catalan version of pizza, though without the cheese. They come with various toppings, including tuna and anchovy.

Preheat the oven to 200°C/400°F/Gas Mark 6, 15 minutes before cooking.

Peel the onion and garlic and chop finely. Heat the oil in a heavy-based saucepan, then fry the onion and garlic for 1–2 minutes until softened, stirring frequently. Add the rosemary sprigs.

Meanwhile, deseed all the peppers and finely chop, then add to the softened onion and cook for a further 5 minutes.

Trim and then finely chop the courgette. Finely chop the tomatoes. Add the courgettes and tomatoes to the saucepan and season to taste. Cover with the lid and cook for 15 minutes, or until cooked and reduced to a thick sauce.

Cool for 5 minutes, then spoon on top of the pizza bases to within 5 mm/¼ inch of the edge. Bake for 15 minutes, or until cooked. Garnish with fresh herbs if liked, and serve.

Coca de Recapte

Cuts into 8 slices

1 pack pizza dough
1 medium aubergine
2 tbsp olive oil
1 red pepper
1 large Spanish onion, peeled and thinly sliced
sea salt

Make the pizza dough as directed on the packet, then roll the dough out on a lightly floured surface and use to line a 20.5 x 25 cm/8 x 10 inch baking tray. Reserve.

Preheat the grill and line the grill rack with kitchen foil. Slice the aubergine thinly and brush one side with oil. Place under the grill and cook for 5 minutes, or until softened. Turn the aubergine slices over, brush with a little more oil and return to the grill. Cook for 3 minutes, or until soft. Remove and drain on absorbent kitchen paper.

Deseed the pepper and cut into quarters. Place on the grill rack and cook for 10 minutes, or until the skin is charred. Remove and allow to cool. Peel, then slice the pepper.

Mix the aubergine, pepper and sliced onion together with salt to taste, together, and place on top of the pizza base. Bake in the preheated oven for 15–20 minutes until the dough is cooked.

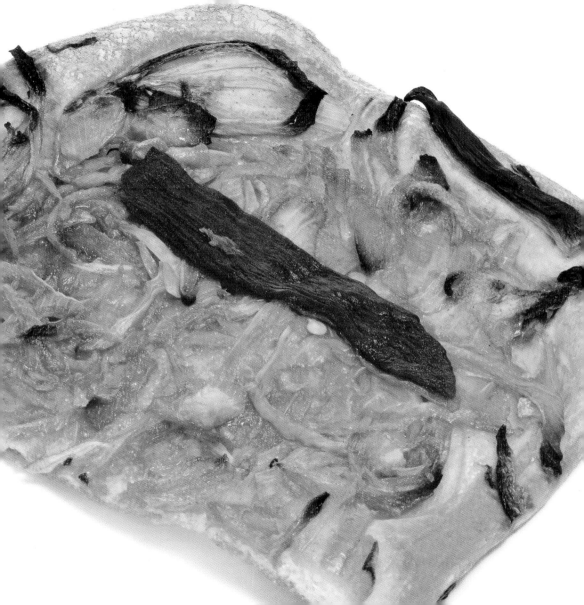

Roasted Red Peppers

Serves 4

4 large red peppers
salt and freshly ground
black pepper
1–2 tbsp Spanish olive oil

Cook's Tip

Any coloured peppers or a
combination of all the peppers
(red, yellow, orange and green)
can be cooked in this way.
Other vegetables can be
cooked liked this too, and are
popular in Spain; try onions,
aubergines and courgettes.

Preheat the oven to 200°C/400°F/Gas Mark 6, 15 minutes before roasting the peppers. If liked, have ready a roasting tin lined with kitchen foil.

Cut the peppers into quarters and discard the seeds together with the membrane. (This is the piece of pepper that the seeds are attached to). Rinse the pepper quarters, then place in the roasting tin, skin-side up. Add seasoning to taste, and drizzle over a little olive oil.

Roast in the preheated oven for 25–30 minutes until the skins are beginning to wrinkle and starting to char. Turn the peppers over occasionally during cooking. When cooked, remove. If wishing to skin, allow to cool for 10 minutes before skinning.

The peppers can be used in salads, stuffings, as a vegetable or pounded down to make a red hummus or other dip. Or they can even be enjoyed on their own!

Red Pepper Salad

Serves 4

4 red peppers
150 ml/¹/₄ pint Spanish olive oil
50 g/2 oz capers in brine
3–4 garlic cloves, peeled
salt and freshly ground
black pepper
1 tsp caster sugar
2 tbsp sherry vinegar
1 tbsp freshly snipped
chives (optional)

Preheat the oven to 200°C/400°F/Gas Mark 6, 15 minutes before roasting the peppers.

Rinse the peppers. Either leave the peppers whole or cut into quarters. If leaving whole, carefully cut a circle around the stalk, then pull and remove the seeds. Alternatively, cut into quarters and remove the seeds.

Place in a roasting tin, pour over 3 tablespoons of the oil, then place in the oven and roast for 15–20 minutes until soft, basting the peppers during roasting. Remove from the oven, reserving the oil.

Drain the capers and rinse thoroughly. Place the peppers and the peeled garlic into a dish and scatter with the capers. Blend the remaining oil with the oil used in cooking, then season to taste with salt and pepper and sprinkle with the sugar and vinegar. Pour over the peppers and leave to marinate for at least 2 hours, longer if time permits, turning the peppers over occasionally.

Serve with the chives, if using, sprinkled over.

Patatas Bravas

Serves 6–8

5 tbsp Spanish olive oil
1 Spanish onion, peeled and
finely chopped
2 garlic cloves, peeled
and crushed
225 g can chopped tomatoes
1 tbsp tomato purée
2 tsp sweet paprika
1/2 tsp chilli powder
1/2 tsp caster sugar
sea salt and freshly ground
black pepper
675 g/1 1/2 lb potatoes
allioli (*see* page 182), for dipping

Preheat the oven to 200°C/400°F/Gas Mark 6, 15 minutes before cooking.

Heat 3 tablespoons of the oil in a heavy-based saucepan, then add the onion and garlic and fry for 5–8 minutes until softened. Add the tomatoes and their juice together with the tomato purée, sweet paprika, chilli powder, sugar and salt. Bring to the boil, stirring, then reduce the heat to a simmer and cook for 10 minutes or until a pulp is formed. Reserve.

Peel the potatoes and cut into small chunks, then pat dry with absorbent kitchen paper. Spread the potatoes in a roasting tin, pour over the remaining oil and turn the potatoes over until they are coated in the oil. Roast in the oven for 40–50 minutes until golden. Add seasoning to taste.

Place the potatoes in a warm serving dish, pour over the prepared sauce and stir to lightly coat the potatoes. Serve with the allioli for dipping.

Classic Tortilla

Serves 8

450 g/1 lb potatoes, peeled
2 tbsp Spanish olive oil
1 Spanish onion, peeled
2–3 garlic cloves, peeled
and crushed
8 medium eggs
sea salt and freshly ground
black pepper
fresh herbs, to garnish (optional)
warm chunky bread, to serve

Cut the potatoes into large chunks, then cook for 12–15 minutes until tender. Drain, leave until cool, then cut into equal-sized chunks and reserve.

Heat the oil in a large, deep frying pan and, when hot, add the onion and garlic and fry gently for 8 minutes, or until softened. Remove and reserve.

Add the potatoes to the pan, stir, then fry gently for 5 minutes, stirring occasionally. Return the onion and garlic to the pan.

Beat the eggs in a bowl, with seasoning to taste and 3 tablespoons water, and slowly pour into the pan. Cook over a medium heat for 5 minutes, or until the base has set, stirring the eggs with a fork while cooking. Reduce the heat to low and cook for a further 10 minutes, or until the eggs are completely set. Test with a knife. If liked, brown the top under a preheated grill.

When set, cool for 10 minutes, then turn out and cut into small chunks. Insert cocktail sticks into the chunks of tortilla to make it easy to pick up. Serve warm or cold, garnished, if liked with herbs, and accompanied with warm bread.

Fried Aubergines

Serves 6

2 medium aubergines
sea salt and freshly ground
black pepper
2 tbsp plain white flour
3 medium free-range eggs
About 150 ml/¼ pint Spanish
olive oil

Trim the aubergines and cut into 5 mm/¼ inch slices. Layer in a colander with salt and leave over a bowl or in the sink (to catch the bitter juices) for at least 30 minutes. Rinse the aubergine slices to remove any salt, and pat each one dry with absorbent kitchen paper.

Season the flour with salt and pepper and place in a dish. Beat the eggs, then pour into a shallow dish.

Heat about 2 tablespoons of the oil in a heavy-based frying pan. Coat an aubergine slice in the flour. Shake off any excess, then dip into the beaten egg. Allow any excess egg to drip back into the bowl.

When the oil is hot, place the egg-coated slices in the oil and fry for 1 minute, or until golden. Using a spatula, turn the slices over and cook for a further 1 minute. Remove, and place on a plate lined with absorbent kitchen paper. Repeat with all the aubergine slices. You can fry about 6 slices together.

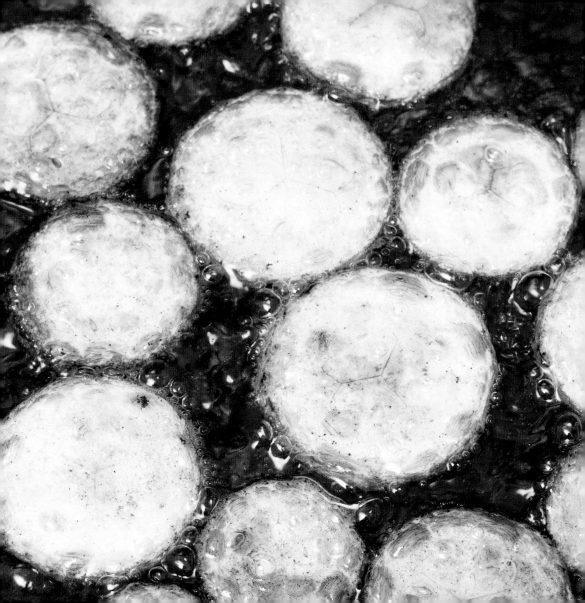

Artichokes in Vinaigrette

Serves 4

4 artichokes
2 tbsp Spanish olive oil
2 tbsp lemon juice
sea salt and freshly ground
black pepper
freshly chopped flat-leaf parsley,
to garnish (optional)

For the vinaigrette

$^1/_2$ tsp dry mustard powder
1 tsp caster sugar or clear honey
2 tsp sherry or white wine vinegar
6 tbsp Spanish virgin olive oil
2 tbsp lemon juice
1 tbsp fresh chopped parsley

Pull off and discard the bottom leaves of the artichokes if they are damaged, then cut the stalk off each artichoke so that it is level with the bottom leaves. Trim the remaining leaves and cut the top so that they are level. Thoroughly wash under cold running water.

Stand the prepared artichokes in a deep saucepan or pot with 7.5 cm/3 inches boiling water. Pour in 1 tablespoon of the oil with the lemon juice and seasoning. Cover with the lid and bring to a gentle boil for 30–40 minutes until a leaf near the centre pulls out easily. When cooked, remove from the pan and stand the artichokes upside down on a rack to drain. Cool, then cut into quarters and place in a dish.

Place all the ingredients for the vinaigrette in a screw-top jar, add seasoning and shake vigorously. Put the artichokes into the vinaigrette in a bowl to marinate, either overnight or until the artichokes have absorbed the the flavour of the vinaigrette. Serve.

Manchego Cheese

Manchego cheese slices
Spanish olive oil

Manchego is a Spanish hard cheese, made from sheep's milk and is only made in the La Mancha region of Spain. It often forms an integral part of any spread of tapas. Much of the taste depends on the age of the cheese, so the older the cheese you choose, the more flavour it will have. Obviously the more mature the cheese, the more expensive it is, but it will be well worth the cost. The colour can vary from white or ivory, to quite a deep yellow/brown and is coated in an unedible rind. It has a creamy texture and the flavour is not very strong, as it still retains the flavour of sheep's milk.

When you buy the Manchego ask for it to be cut as a section of a round. When serving, the traditional way is to serve cut into triangular slices, with the rind still on at one end. Sometimes olive oil is drizzled over the cheese.

Tortilla Montaditos

Serves 4

225 g/8 oz potatoes, peeled
1 tbsp Spanish olive oil
1 medium Spanish onion, peeled
1–2 garlic cloves, peeled
and crushed
4 medium eggs
sea salt and freshly ground
black pepper
warm chunky bread
fresh mint sprigs,
to garnish (optional)

Cut the potatoes into small chunks, then cook for 10–12 minutes until tender. Drain, leave until cool and reserve.

Heat the oil in a medium-sized frying pan and, when hot, add the onion and garlic. Fry gently for 8 minutes, or until softened. Remove and reserve.

Add the potatoes to the pan, stir, then fry gently for 5 minutes, stirring occasionally. Return the onion and garlic to the pan.

Beat the eggs in a bowl, with seasoning to taste and 2 tablespoons of water, and slowly pour into the pan. Cook over a medium heat for 5 minutes, or until the base has set, stirring the eggs with a fork while cooking. Reduce to a low heat and cook for a further 10 minutes, or until the eggs are completely set. Test with a knife. If liked, brown the top under a preheated grill.

When set, cool for 10 minutes, then turn out and cut into 8 small slices. Cut the bread into 8 slices. Place a slice of tortilla on top of each bread slice and garnish with a mint sprig. If liked, insert cocktail sticks into the tortilla slices and bread to make it easy to pick up. Serve warm or cold.

Manchego Montaditos

Serves 4

175 g/6 oz Manchego cheese
75 g/3 oz sun-dried tomatoes in oil,
or 75 g/3 oz dried quince in oil
8 slices of country bread, or
4 soft rolls
2 tbsp Spanish olive oil
8 pitted black olives, sliced

Place the cheese on a chopping board, if preferred, then slice thinly, taking care that the slices do not fall apart when moved.

Drain the sun-dried tomatoes or quince and if liked, soak in a little warm water to remove some of the oil. Or simply pat them dry with absorbent kitchen paper to remove the excess oil.

Toast the bread if liked, and if using rolls, cut them in half. Drizzle the toast or rolls with the olive oil. Place a slice of toast or the base of the roll on a serving platter and arrange a layer of cheese, sun-dried tomatoes or quince and a little sliced black olive. Serve.

Tortilla Red Pepper Montaditos

Serves 4

225 g/8 oz potatoes
1 medium Spanish onion
1–2 garlic cloves
1 tbsp Spanish olive oil
4 medium eggs
sea salt and freshly ground
black pepper
8 small 1 cm/¹/₂ inch thick slices
country bread,
toasted (optional)
1–2 tbsp Spanish extra virgin
olive oil
2 small red peppers, deseeded,
skinned (*see* page 130) and cut
into quarters

Peel the potatoes and cut into large pieces. Cook for 12–15 minutes until tender. Drain; leave until cool then cut into equal-sized chunks and reserve. Peel and thinly slice the onion and garlic.

Heat the olive oil in a 20.5 cm/8 inch frying pan and, when hot, add the onion and garlic. Gently fry for 8 minutes, or until softened. Remove and reserve.

Add the potatoes to the pan then stir and fry gently for 5 minutes stirring occasionally. Return the onion and garlic to the pan.

Beat the eggs in a bowl, with seasoning to taste and 3 tablespoons of water, and slowly pour into the pan. Cook over a medium heat for 5 minutes or until the base has set, stirring the eggs with a fork while cooking.

Reduce to a low heat and cook for a further 10 minutes or until the eggs are completely set. Test with a knife.

When set, cool for 10 minutes, then turn out and cut into pieces.

Toast the bread if liked, and drizzle over a little extra virgin olive oil. Top with the tortilla and a quarter of the red pepper and serve.

Mushroom, Olive Potato Tortilla

Serves 4

300 g/10 oz potatoes, peeled and
cut into large pieces
4 tbsp Spanish olive oil
1 Spanish onion, peeled and cut
into wedges or pieces
2–3 garlic cloves, peeled
and sliced
225 g/8 oz field or chestnut
mushrooms, wiped and cut
into pieces
sea salt and freshly ground
black pepper
50 g/2 oz olives, pitted
8 medium eggs
warm chunky bread, to serve

Cook the potatoes for 15 minutes, or until tender. Drain; leave until cool then cut into equal-sized chunks and reserve.

Heat 2 tablespoons of the oil in a frying pan and, when hot, add the onion and garlic and gently fry for 3 minutes. Add the mushrooms and continue to cook for a further 5 minutes. Add to the potatoes, together with seasoning to taste and the olives.

Heat a little of the remaining oil in a 15 cm/6 inch frying pan and add a quarter of the potato and mushroom mixture. Beat the eggs in a bowl, with seasoning to taste and 3 tablespoons of water, and slowly pour in a quarter of the eggs. Cook over a medium heat for 3 minutes, or until the base has set, stirring the eggs with a fork while cooking.

Reduce to a low heat and cook for a further 5–7 minutes until the eggs are completely set. Test with a knife. If liked, brown the top under a preheated grill. Repeat three more times with the rest of the potatoes, mushrooms and eggs. Serve with warm bread.

Banderillas

Serves 4

1 red pepper, skinned
(*see* page 130)
175 g/6 oz green olives, pitted
125 g/4 oz pickled garlic

Food Fact

These easy to make kebabs or banderillas get their name from the barbed darts used during a bullfight. Fortunately, these 'kebabs' are not dangerous but very tasty, and are great served with an aperitif.

Cut the red pepper into small pieces and drain both the olives and garlic. Thread the red pepper, olives and garlic onto cocktail sticks. Place on a platter and serve.

Other ingredients can be used if liked. Try olives that are pitted and stuffed with almonds, anchovies or pimentos. Or use anchovies which are rolled up to form a ball, small cocktail onions, chunks of tuna, cooked peeled prawns, cubes of cheese or small pieces of artichokes.

Salad ingredients can also be used, such as cherry tomatoes, spring onion or cucumber as well as fruits, including pineapple, apple, grapes and melon. For a party, you can serve a selection of these using lots of different ingredients.

Goat's Cheese Pepper Montaditos

Serves 4

8 slices of country bread or
4 soft rolls
2 tbsp Spanish olive oil
2 large tomatoes
175 g/6 oz goat's cheese
2 tbsp freshly chopped herbs,
such as flat-leaf parsley
or chives
4–8 Padrón peppers

Toast the bread if liked, and if using rolls, cut in half. Drizzle the toast or rolls with the olive oil.

Place a slice of toast or the base of the roll on a serving platter. Place a slice of tomato on top and sprinkle with a little chopped herb. Top with a slice of cheese and a further sprinkle of herbs. Finish with 1 or 2 pieces of the Padrón peppers and serve.

Catalan Roasted Vegetable Salad

Serves 4–6

2 medium onions
3–4 garlic cloves
1 small aubergine
1 red pepper
1 yellow pepper
4 firm but ripe tomatoes
2 tbsp Spanish olive oil
2 tbsp lemon juice
1 tbsp sherry vinegar
1 tsp Spanish paprika

Preheat the oven to 180°C/350°F/Gas Mark 4, 10 minutes before cooking.

Peel the onions and garlic and leave whole. Trim the stalk from the aubergine, then rinse the aubergine and peppers. Place the onions in a roasting tin and cook for 10 minutes. Reserve 1 garlic clove and add all the vegetables, including the tomatoes, to the onions in the tin. Drizzle with 1 tablespoon of the oil and continue to cook for a further 20–25 minutes until the vegetables are tender. Turn the vegetables over a couple of times during cooking. Remove from the oven and leave until cool enough to handle.

Cut the onion into small wedges. Chop the garlic if liked, and cut the aubergine into small chunks. Cut the peppers into quarters, discard the seeds, then chop into small pieces. Reserve half the tomatoes and skin, then cut the remaining tomatoes into pieces. Place all the prepared vegetables in a serving dish.

Place all the remaining ingredients in a food processor together with the reserved tomatoes and blend to form a smooth dressing. Pour over the vegetables and serve.

Chickpeas with Spinach

Serves 4

6 tbsp Spanish olive oil
450 g/1 lb fresh spinach,
thoroughly rinsed
sea salt and freshly ground
black pepper
75 g/3 oz piece crusty bread,
crusts removed and cut into
small chunks
3 garlic cloves, peeled and sliced
2 tbsp red wine vinegar
$^1/_2$ tsp ground cumin
$^1/_2$ tsp crushed chillies
225 g/8 oz dried and cooked
chickpeas or 2 x 400 g can
chickpeas, drained and rinsed
150 ml/$^1/_4$ pint ready-made
tomato sauce
1–2 tbsp fresh lemon juice
fried bread, to serve (optional)

Heat 3 tablespoons of the olive oil in a large saucepan and add the spinach, together with a little salt. Cover with the lid and cook for 3–4 minutes until the spinach starts to wilt. Drain and reserve.

Heat a further 2 tablespoons of oil in the pan and fry the bread for 4–5 minutes, turning the bread over until they are golden. Add the garlic and cook for a further few minutes.

Place the bread mixture in a food processor together with the red wine vinegar, and process until a paste is formed. Scrape the mixture back into the pan and add the ground cumin, crushed chillies and the chickpeas and tomato sauce. Add seasoning to taste with the lemon juice and heat until thoroughly hot, and the chickpeas have absorbed the flavours. Season with salt and pepper, stir in the spinach and serve with fried bread, if liked.

Mushroom Pumpkin Montaditos

Serves 4

350 g/12 oz piece pumpkin
2 medium onions
125 g/4 oz shiitake or
field mushrooms
6–8 tbsp Spanish olive oil
sea salt and freshly ground
black pepper
8 country bread slices, or
4 soft rolls
2 tbsp Spanish extra virgin olive oil

Peel the pumpkin, discard the seeds and cut into equal-sized pieces. Bring a medium-sized saucepan half filled with water to the boil, and cook the pumpkin for 10–12 minutes until tender. Drain and allow to dry.

Peel the onions, keeping the root intact, and cut into wedges. Reserve. Wipe the mushrooms and cut into wedges. Heat 1 tablespoon of the olive oil and fry the onions, stirring occasionally for 8–10 minutes until turning golden, adding a little more oil if necessary. Remove from the pan and reserve.

Heat a further 2 tablespoons of the olive oil in the pan and fry the mushrooms for 5–6 minutes until cooked, then drain and reserve. Add more oil if required.

Add a further 2 tablespoons of the oil to the pan and fry the pumpkin in the oil until golden and beginning to crisp round the edges. Drain.

Toast the bread, if liked or if using rolls, cut in half. Drizzle the toast or rolls with the extra virgin olive oil.

Place the bread (or toast) or the base of the roll on a serving platter and top with the onion, mushroom and pumpkin wedges, then serve.

Spinach with Pine Nuts

Serves 4

675 g/1¹/₂ lb fresh spinach
2–4 tbsp Spanish extra virgin olive oil
4 small garlic cloves
75 g/3 oz pine nuts
sea salt and freshly ground black pepper
1 tbsp butter, softened

Thoroughly wash the spinach, discarding any tough stalks, then drain off the excess water and place in a large saucepan. Place over a medium heat and cover with the lid. Bring to the boil then reduce the heat and simmer for 5 minutes, or until the spinach has wilted and is tender.

Drain the spinach, squeezing out the water, then chop coarsely. Reserve until ready to cook.

Heat the oil in a frying pan and fry the garlic and pine nuts for 4–5 minutes until the nuts are golden. Add the reserved spinach and stir together. Heat for 2–3 minutes until the spinach is hot. Add seasoning to taste. Spoon into a warm serving dish and dot with the butter, then serve.

Sautéed Vegetable Montaditos

Serves 4

2 medium Spanish onions
4 garlic cloves
2 red peppers
2 yellow peppers
2 orange peppers
1 red chilli
3–4 tbsp Spanish olive oil
sea salt and freshly ground
black pepper
1 baguette large enough to cut
into 8 slices
2 tbsp Spanish extra virgin olive
oil, for drizzling (optional)

Peel the onions without cutting through the root. Cut in half from tip to the root, then slice. Peel and chop the garlic cloves. Cut the peppers into quarters and discard the seeds and membrane, then slice into strips. Cut the chilli in half and discard the seeds, then cut into thin strips.

Heat the olive oil in a frying pan and add all the vegetables. Cook, stirring frequently for 25–30 minutes until the vegetables are tender and the skins are beginning to blister. Season to taste.

Cut the baguette into 8 slices and drizzle with a little extra virgin olive oil, if using. Top with the cooked vegetables and serve while still warm.

Sweet Snacks and Dessert Tapas

This chapter is filled with a great selection of desserts for anyone with a sweet tooth. The simply divine yet equally show-stopping Crème Caramel is a great accompaniment to any tapas selection. For a more filling option, you could go for the traditionally warming Rice Pudding and serve it with Catalan Biscuits. Those in search of a sweet snack should try Churros (Spanish doughnuts), which are best enjoyed with a mug of hot chocolate.

Churros

Serves 4–6

300 ml/¹/₂ pint water
5 tbsp sunflower oil, plus extra
for frying
1 tsp ground cinnamon
finely grated zest of 1 small lemon
200 g/7 oz plain white flour
pinch salt
1 medium egg
oil, for deep-frying
1 tbsp icing sugar, for dusting

Pour the water into a heavy-based saucepan and pour in the oil. Add half the cinnamon with the lemon zest and bring to the boil. Sift the flour with the salt and when the water comes to the boil, tip in the flour and beat well with a wooden spoon over a low heat. Continue to beat until a ball forms in the centre of the pan and the sides are clean of any mixture. Leave to cool for about 5 minutes, then beat in the egg.

When ready to cook, heat the oil for deep-frying in a deep-fat fryer and heat to 180°C/350°F. Have ready a plate lined with absorbent kitchen paper.

Spoon the mixture into a large piping bag fitted with a large nozzle. Only fill the bag to half full, otherwise the mixture will be difficult to pipe.

Once the oil has reached temperature, pipe 7.5 cm/3 inch lengths into the hot oil and cook for 3–4 minutes until golden. Using a slotted spoon, remove the churros carefully from the oil and drain on kitchen paper. Repeat until all the mixture has been used. Dust with the icing sugar mixed with the remaining cinnamon and serve warm.

Rice Pudding

Serves 4

25 g/1 oz unsalted butter, plus for
extra for greasing
50 g/2 oz pudding (short-grain) rice
2–3 tsp sugar
1 tsp ground cinnamon
600 ml/1 pint milk, plus extra
if necessary
cinnamon sticks, to decorate

Cook's Tip

If liked, the ground cinnamon can
be replaced with 1 tablespoon of
finely grated orange or lemon
zest. Or stir in 25 g/1 oz dried
fruit such as apricots, sultanas
or raisins.

Preheat the oven to 150°C/300°F/Gas Mark 2, 20 minutes
before cooking.

Lightly butter a 900 ml/1½ pint ovenproof dish. Rinse the rice
lightly in a sieve and then place in the dish.

Sprinkle with the sugar and a little of the ground cinnamon.
Pour over the milk and stir, then sprinkle with the remaining
ground cinnamon.

Place on a baking sheet (this will make it easier to remove from
the oven when it is hot). Cook for 30 minutes, then remove and
stir. Return to the oven and cook for a further 30 minutes, then
remove and stir again. Return the pudding to the oven and
cook for a further 45 minutes–1 hour. If liked, remove the skin
towards the end of cooking.

Add a little extra milk if the pudding is too thick for your
liking. Serve warm in individual bowls, with a cinnamon stick
to decorate.

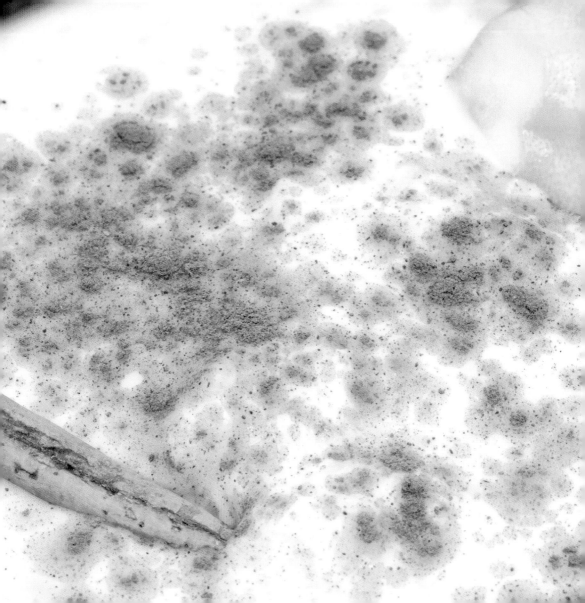

Crema Catalana

Serves 6

500 ml/18 fl oz double cream
1 tsp vanilla extract
125 g/4 oz caster sugar
6 medium egg yolks
6 heaped teaspoons
demerara sugar
sweet biscuits, to serve

Preheat the oven to 150°C/300°F/Gas Mark 2. Pour the cream into a heavy-based saucepan and add the vanilla extract. Place over a medium heat and bring to the boil. Reduce the heat to a simmer and cook for 5 minutes.

Meanwhile, beat the sugar and egg yolks together until pale and creamy. Return the cream to the boil then whisk into the egg and sugar. Continue to whisk until the mixture thickens.

Strain the mixture through a fine sieve and pour into 6 x 150 ml/ ¼ pint ramekins or ovenproof dishes. Leave a space at the top where the sugar can be sprinkled.

Place the dishes in a roasting tin and carefully pour in boiling water to come halfway up the sides of the dishes. Take care while placing in the oven and cook for 35–40 minutes until the custard is set, but still has a wobble in the middle. Remove from the oven and cool, then place in the refrigerator to chill overnight.

When ready to serve, sprinkle with the demerara sugar and place under a preheated grill, turning as necessary until the sugar has lightly caramelized. Chill in the refrigerator for a few minutes, then serve with sweet biscuits.

Crème Caramel

Serves 4

125 g/4 oz caster sugar
150 ml/¹/₄ pint water
3 medium eggs
1 tsp vanilla extract
450 ml/³/₄ pint milk

Preheat the oven to 160°C/325°F/Gas Mark 3, 10 minutes before cooking. Place all but 1 tablespoon of the sugar in a heavy-based saucepan and add the water. Bring to the boil over a medium heat, stirring frequently in order to dissolve the sugar. When the sugar is completely dissolved, bring to the boil, then boil steadily until the syrup becomes golden.

Remove from the heat and quickly pour into 4 x 150 ml/¹/₄ pint ramekins or ovenproof dishes. Working quickly, swirl the syrup around the dishes until they are lightly coated. It is advisable to use a thick cloth, as the dishes will be hot. Place in a roasting tin and reserve.

Beat the eggs together with the remaining sugar and the vanilla extract. Warm the milk slightly, then whisk or beat into the eggs. Carefully strain into the dishes in the roasting tin. Carefully pour in sufficient boiling water to go halfway up the sides of the dishes. Take care while placing in the oven and cook for 30–35 minutes until the custard has set and feels firm on the top. Remove and cool, then place in the refrigerator and leave to chill, preferably overnight.

When ready to serve, run a knife around the edge of each pudding and invert onto a serving dish.

Magdalenas

Makes about 9–10

2 medium eggs, beaten
125 g/4 oz caster sugar, plus extra
for sprinkling
125 g/4 oz unsalted butter
finely grated zest and juice from
1 large lemon
1 tbsp milk
125 g/4 oz plain white flour
2 level tsp baking powder

Preheat the oven to 190°C/375°F/Gas Mark 5, 10 minutes before baking and line a bun tin with 9–10 paper cases.

Beat the eggs and the sugar together in a medium mixing bowl until creamy. Melt the butter and allow to cool before slowly beating into the egg mixture. Mix well.

Stir in the lemon zest together with the lemon juice and milk. Sift the flour and baking powder together then slowly stir into the egg mixture. Stir well, until the mixture is thoroughly mixed together to form a thick batter.

Spoon the batter into the paper cases, filling just over half full and bake in the oven for 15–20 minutes until the cakes are well risen and golden and feel firm when touched lightly with a clean finger. Sprinkle with little sugar and serve warm or cold. Store in an airtight tin.

Tarta de Santiago

Serves 8–10

oil for oiling
175 g/6 oz unsalted butter
175 g/6 oz caster sugar
few drops almond extract
3 medium eggs, beaten
125 g/4 oz self-raising flour
50 g/2 oz ground almonds
1 tbsp cooled boiled
water (optional)
75 g/3 oz self-raising flour
1 tbsp flaked almonds
1–2 tsp icing sugar

Preheat the oven to 180°C/350°F/Gas Mark 4, 10 minutes before baking. Line the base of a 20.5 cm/8 inch cake tin with greaseproof paper or baking parchment, then oil the base and sides.

Place the butter and sugar in a mixing bowl and beat until creamy, then beat in the almond extract.

Slowly beat in the eggs a little at a time, beating well after each addition and adding 1 tablespoon of flour. When all the egg has bean added, stir in any remaining flour and then the ground almonds. Add the cooled boiled water if the mixture is stiff.

Spoon into the prepared tin and smooth the top. Sprinkle with the flaked almonds, place on the middle shelf in the oven and bake for 30–40 minutes until cooked and a skewer inserted in the centre comes out clean. Remove from the oven and allow to cool before removing from the tin and discarding the lining paper. Sift the icing sugar over the top and serve cut into wedges.

Lenten Cakes (Torrijas)

Serves 4

1 stale white baguette, or 4–5
slices stale white bread
175 ml/6 fl oz milk
1 medium egg
1/2 tsp vanilla extract
5–6 tbsp vegetable oil
2 tbsp caster sugar and 1 tsp
ground cinnamon, for sprinkling
honey, for drizzling (optional)

Heat a heavy-based frying pan until hot. Cook the bread in the pan for 1 minute, turn over, cook for a further minute then remove from the pan. Repeat until all the bread has been cooked.

Pour the milk into a mixing bowl. Beat the egg and vanilla extract into the milk. Pour about 2 tablespoons of oil into the frying pan, making sure there is sufficient to cover the base of the pan and heat on medium. Be careful that the oil does not burn.

Dip the bread into the milk and egg mixture and quickly turn it over with a fork. Remove from the bowl and allow excess milk to drip into the bowl. Cook each side in the frying pan for 1 minute, until golden. Repeat with the remaining slices.

Remove the bread from the pan and place on a plate. If using sliced bread, cut into smaller pieces. Sprinkle the top with sugar and ground cinnamon. If you prefer, drizzle honey over the top. Serve.

Bunuelos de Cuaresma

Serves 4–6

250 ml/9 fl oz milk
90 g/3¹/₂ oz unsalted butter,
chopped, at room temperature
finely grated zest of 1 lemon
pinch salt
125 g/4 oz plain flour, sifted
3 medium eggs
vegetable oil, for deep-frying
1 tsp ground cinnamon
75 g/3 oz caster sugar
300 ml/¹/₂ pint ready-made
vanilla custard

Place the milk, butter, lemon zest and salt in a pan and bring to the boil. Stir in the flour. Reduce the heat to medium and cook for 2 minutes or until the mixture starts to form into a ball. Remove from the heat. Add the eggs, one at a time, mixing well after each addition. Transfer to a bowl, cover and refrigerate for 30 minutes to cool.

Fill a deep-fat fryer or large saucepan one-third full with vegetable oil for deep-frying and heat to 160°C/325°F, or until a cube of bread dropped into the oil turns golden in 15 seconds. When the oil has reached the correct temperature, drop tablespoonfuls of the batter into the oil and fry, turning halfway, for 4 minutes, or until golden and cooked through. Remove with a slotted spoon and drain on absorbent kitchen paper.

Spoon the custard into a piping bag fitted with a large nozzle. Insert the nozzle into the base of a fritter and fill with the custard. Repeat. Combine the cinnamon and sugar in a bowl, then roll the fritters in the cinnamon mixture and serve.

Valencian Pumpkin Pies (Pastissets)

Makes about 10

225 g/8 oz prepared
shortcrust pastry
plain flour, for dusting
2 large eggs, plus 1 yolk
75 g/3 oz soft brown sugar
1 tsp ground cinnamon
^{1}/$_2$ level teaspoon freshly
grated nutmeg
^{1}/$_2$ tsp ground allspice
^{1}/$_2$ tsp ground cloves
^{1}/$_2$ tsp ground ginger
300 ml/^{1}/$_2$ pint double cream
400g can pumpkin flesh
1 small egg, beaten, for brushing

Preheat the oven to 180°C/350°F/Gas Mark 4, 10 minutes before baking.

Roll the pastry out on a lightly floured surface and cut out 10 x 10 cm/4 inch rounds. Reserve.

Whisk the eggs and extra yolk together in a large bowl. Reserve.

Place the sugar, spices and the cream in a heavy-based saucepan and bring to simmering point, giving it a whisk to mix everything together, then pour over the eggs and whisk again.

Purée the pumpkin flesh if chunky, then add to the cream mixture, still whisking to blend everything thoroughly.

Place spoonfuls of the mixture onto the prepared pastry rounds and brush the edges with egg. Fold over to form a half moon shape, place on a baking sheet and brush lightly with more egg.

Bake in the oven for 20 minutes or until cooked and golden brown. Remove and cool before serving.

Catalan Biscuits (Panellets)

Makes about 20–24

butter or oil, for greasing
450 g/1 lb small
potatoes, unpeeled
140 g/5 oz ground almonds
200 g/7 oz caster sugar
few drops of almond extract
140 g/5 oz chopped almonds,
plus extra for sprinkling
1 medium egg white, beaten

Preheat the oven to 180°C/350°F/Gas Mark 4, 10 minutes before baking. Lightly oil or butter two baking sheets. Reserve.

Wash the potatoes and place in a saucepan. Cover with water and bring to the boil. Cover with the lid, reduce the heat to a simmer and cook for 20 minutes, or until the potatoes are tender when pierced with a fork. Drain and allow to cool. When cool enough to handle, peel then mash.

Stir the ground almonds into the potatoes, then stir in the caster sugar, almond extract and nuts and mix well to form a thick dough. Cut off small pieces of dough and roll into balls and place on the prepared baking sheets.

Brush with the beaten egg white and sprinkle with extra almonds. Bake in the oven for 10–15 minutes until golden. Remove and allow to cool before serving.

Wine Doughnuts (Roscos de Vino)

Serves about 18

200 g/7 oz caster sugar
300 ml/¹/₂ pint vegetable oil
225 g/8 oz butter or margarine
1¹/₂ tsp baking powder
225 ml/8 fl oz white wine
1 tsp anise extract, or use
vanilla extract
200 g/7 oz plain flour
1–2 tbsp granulated sugar,
for sprinkling

Preheat the oven to 160°C/325°F/Gas Mark 3, 10 minutes before cooking.

Place the sugar, vegetable oil and butter or margarine into a mixing bowl and mix together. Add the baking powder and beat until mixed thoroughly. Slowly pour in the white wine and anise or vanilla extract and mix well, stirring in the flour a spoonful at a time. The mixture should seem dry or crumbly. You may want to use your hand to mix the dough together towards the end of adding the last amount of flour.

Roll the dough into a rope about 5 mm/¹/₄ inch thick on a chopping board. Cut into pieces about 10 cm/4 inches long and join the two ends to form individual doughnuts or rings.

Carefully place on a dry baking sheet and bake in the oven for 15–18 minutes until they become a golden colour. Be careful not to burn the bases. While still warm, either sprinkle the tops with sugar or roll the whole pastry in the sugar to coat. Serve.

Index